FIGHTING
FOR YOUR
MILITARY
MARRIAGE

FIGHTING
FOR YOUR
MILITARY
MARRIAGE

7
CRITICAL SKILLS
TO ENSURE MISSION
SUCCESS WITH YOUR
LIFEMATE

MICHAEL AND MYRA HOLMES

purposely
created
PUBLISHING

FIGHTING FOR YOUR MILITARY MARRIAGE
Published by Purposely Created Publishing Group™
Copyright © 2020 Michael and Myra Holmes
All rights reserved.

This book is not intended as a substitute for the medical advice of any medical provider (e.g., physician, physician assistant, nurse practitioner, or nurse), or the psychological and mental health advice of licensed and certified mental health providers (e.g., psychiatrists, psychologists, marriage and family therapists and counselors). The authors also encourage readers to seek spiritual guidance and counseling from their chaplain, pastor, priest, rabbi, etc. The authors' intent is to support and assist you in reaching your own goals, but your success depends primarily on your own commitment and follow-through. We cannot predict and we do not guarantee that you will attain a particular result. Your results depend on your unique background, dedication, desire, motivation, actions, and numerous other factors. There are no guarantees as to the specific results you can expect to see from applying the information documented in this book.

Unless otherwise indicated, scripture quotations are from the Holy Bible, King James Version. All rights reserved. Scriptures marked ESV are taken from English Standard Version®. Copyright © 2001 by Crossway, a publishing ministry of Good News Publishers. All rights reserved. Scriptures marked NIV are taken from the New International Version®. Copyright © 1973, 1978, 1984, 2011 by Biblica, Inc.™ All rights reserved. Scriptures marked NKJV are taken from the New King James Version®. Copyright © 1982 by Thomas Nelson. All rights reserved.

Printed in the United States of America
ISBN: 978-1-64484-208-9

*A portion of the proceeds from the sale of this book
will be donated to Operation Homefront.*

Contents

Acknowledgments

Fighting for Your Military Marriage has been a long time coming. It was inspired by our mastermind support team, led by Lamar and Ronnie Tyler, and the military men, women, and their families who sacrifice so much for this great nation.

We would be remiss if we didn't acknowledge the impact of Michael's parents, Cecil and Melynda Holmes, and Myra's parents, Odell and Joann Williamson (deceased). Their love, perseverance, and model for marriage provided a solid example for us to follow. In addition to our parents, we were blessed to have Dan and Gwen White as close friends and mentors during the early years of our marriage.

We appreciate Jeanna Hudgins and Vivian Walker for accepting our request to review our manuscript. They provided the precious feedback that shaped this book.

A special thanks to our book writing coaches Aya Fubara Eneli, Esq., CEO of Aya Eneli International, and Candice Davis, CEO of Go Write Something (candiceldavis.com). These talented ladies helped us organize our thoughts and guided us through the process of birthing this book.

Foreword

After nearly forty years as husband and wife, Michael and Myra Holmes are still obviously very much in love with each other. They hold hands more than any other couple we know. When you see one, you can expect to see the other. Since Michael's retirement from the Air Force, they not only spend their free time together, they've also built a business together. They're each other's greatest support, biggest cheerleader, and best friend. Michael and Myra provide a real world example of how fulfilling and how much fun marriage can be if you're willing to put in the work. Their relationship exemplifies "ride or die."

We first met this dynamic couple when they attended one of our Black and Married with Kids events. They were among many couples who showed up and introduced themselves to us, but Michael and Myra *kept* showing up. They regularly came out to support us and our mission to provide positive images of marriage to our community and to empower married couples. What impressed us even more was that, though they'd been married longer than most of us, they enthusiastically engaged in the activities to further enrich their own marriage. They've never rested on their success as a couple or as marriage coaches. They never take for granted what they have in each other.

As we developed both a professional relationship and a friendship with Michael and Myra, we and the people in our circle began to see them as a perfect couple with a perfect marriage. They seemed to have it all figured out, so when Michael shared in a meeting that their marriage had been on rocky ground in the early years, the revelation practically leveled the room. Among our mutual friends and colleagues, people often talk about them as "relationship goals," and most of us assumed they'd always had the intimate, caring relationship they have today. Hearing their story of overcoming serious challenges in their marriage gave everyone a sense of hope for their own relationship and for marriage as an institution.

As the founders of the largest independent African American marriage and parenting site on the internet, we've spent a decade producing content and events to help couples nurture and strengthen their marriages. We've also built relationships with many professionals who work as marriage coaches, counselors, and mentors. The professionals in our community are good, but Michael and Myra Holmes stand out among those who are great.

They have a passion for mentoring couples, and the knowledge they offer can help strengthen, heal, and restore marriages from all walks of life. At the same time, as a retired Colonel and longtime military spouse, they also have a unique perspective on making the most of marriage and family while navigating the challenges of life in the military.

Serving in the military shouldn't mean you have to sacrifice your marriage—and when you have the right tools, successful military service doesn't have to come at that high price. Those tools are found in this book. *Fighting for Your Military Marriage* should be mandatory reading for military couples across the country and around the globe.

Lamar and Ronnie Tyler
Founders of BlackandMarriedwithKids.com

Introduction

You *can* have a strong, loving, passionate marriage that lasts. You and your spouse can overcome the challenges in your relationship, live up to your vows, and love each other more with each passing year. You can do this even if one or both of you has messed up in the past. You can do this while you're raising children, working multiple jobs, or caring for elderly parents. You can even have the marriage you once dreamed you'd have while you manage the demands military life places on your family at the same time. We know this for a fact because we've done it, and we've helped many other couples do it too.

We've been married since May of 1980 (nearly four decades as we write this) and raised three daughters together. We spend most of our free time together because we enjoy each other's company so much. We work and play together. We share inside jokes and we're each the other's most trusted confidante. Whether we're together or apart, we speak highly of each other, and when we celebrate each other, we mean every word we say. All these years after saying, "I do," we're still in love, still attracted to each other, and still having a good time. Today, we lead marriage seminars and workshops and provide marriage coaching and mentoring for couples.

It probably looks to many people like we have, and have always had, a "perfect" marriage. But nothing could be further from the truth. We've enjoyed our share of mountain-top experiences, but we've also struggled through our fair share of dark valleys. We did the work to build a strong relationship, a loving friendship, and an enduring marriage. We made the effort to become true lifemates, all while the usual challenges of marriage were amplified by the unique demands of life as a military family over a twenty-seven-year Air Force career. As we pushed through and overcame each challenge together, we stumbled upon a clear path to marriage success.

Many sources report that one in every two American marriages ends in divorce. That's a whopping fifty percent failure rate! Those are tough odds that can weigh heavily and create a sense of hopelessness in people thinking about holy matrimony, especially couples going through rough times. It's discouraging to see so many marriages ending in divorce, especially when those failed marriages involve our brothers and sisters in arms. Fortunately, it doesn't have to be that way. We've dedicated the second half of our lives to helping couples like you improve the odds that your marriage will not only be successful, but will thrive, be filled with passion and love, and grow stronger and better with time.

We want you to free yourself from the tyranny of divorce statistics. Statistical probabilities work well to determine how often a coin flip will come up heads, where lightning will strike next, or your chances of winning the lottery, but your marriage isn't a random act. God gave you the ability to think and the freedom and power to choose.

If you want your marriage to survive in today's world of distraction, temptation, and immediate gratification, you and your spouse need to make a joint commitment to fight for your relationship. You must focus on your decision to love one another even when it's not easy. Marriage is hard work. You have to decide to uphold the vows you made to each other before God, your family, and all your witnesses. These choices will boost your chances of success from fifty percent to nearly one hundred percent.

During our initial coaching sessions with clients, we always ask the couple to tell us the story of how they met. For some couples, the details of their story flow naturally. They recreate the sequence of events with great specificity. They recall what time of day it was, who was there, what music was playing, the excitement of the first time they held hands, and the passion they felt when they first kissed. After they share their stories, we share ours.

While I (Myra) was a high school senior, Michael and my sister were at North Carolina Central University together. My sister told me about this guy she wanted me to meet, but Michael was away every time my family and I visited the campus, so we didn't connect that year. Our paths finally crossed, early in my college freshman year, after I enrolled at the same school. As a new freshman, I was a little anxious about college life. Making new friends, finding my way around campus, getting used to the demands of college-level classes—it was a lot to juggle.

One evening, my sister introduced me to Michael. We were in the cafeteria, and he sat down across from me. Right away, I thought he was cute, and then he asked me if I wanted his ice cream. He didn't know it, but I *love* ice cream, and he earned two points for that move. As the evening progressed, the cafeteria cleared out until only Michael and I and one of my dormmates remained. Finally, my dormmate told us she felt like a third wheel, and she headed back to her room. Michael didn't miss a beat. The moment we were alone, he asked me, "Would you like a tour of the campus?"

On that September night when I (Michael) first met my future wife, the weather was perfect. The temperature and humidity were just right. The moon was full, and there I was, spending time with the most beautiful woman I'd ever seen. Myra accepted my invitation to tour the campus, and as we walked, I asked her tons of questions. Where was she from? What was her major? What did she see herself doing after college? In turn, I shared some of my experiences as a military brat (a term military dependents embrace with honor). I talked about living in Germany from third grade to sixth grade. I told her about the three different high schools I attended in Dover, Delaware; Bossier, Louisiana; and on Clark Air Force Base in the Republic of the Philippines.

By the time we'd gotten a quarter of the way around our college campus, we were holding hands. The more I talked, the more Myra giggled. Eventually we circled the entire campus and returned to her dorm. I'd never experienced a night like that, and I didn't want it to end. We stood there for a few minutes, facing each other. When my hand "accidentally" brushed her side, Myra jumped and I asked her, "Are you ticklish?" She said, "A little bit." And that's when I reached out and tickled her in for our first kiss. We've been a couple ever since that night. Sometimes we say it was love at first sight, but in reality, even though there was a strong mutual attraction and a definite chemistry, it wasn't love yet.

The spark ignited between us that night turned into a relationship, and eventually, into marriage. However, unlike in the movies, we didn't go straight to happily ever after. I (Michael) made many mistakes over the first decade of our marriage. I attribute some of my mistakes to immaturity, but most were the result of a lack of knowledge. Marriage doesn't come with an instruction manual, technical order, or flight plan, and I was figuring things out as I went. During that time, I was often guilty of taking Myra for granted. However, when I came terrifyingly close to losing my wife after a life-threatening miscarriage early in our marriage, I got my wake-up call. Having faced the possibility of a life without her, I became highly motivated to change my behavior. I committed to loving Myra more and more every day. I was determined to treat her like my queen and prove to her that I was worthy of her forgiveness and her love.

As the years passed and we moved to different parts of the country, we reconnected from time to time with friends who'd gotten married around the same time we did. Unfortunately, a significant number of those marriages had ended. Seeing this led us to ask a key question. *Why did our marriage succeed while theirs failed?* Answering this question led us to mentor other couples, and we eventually became marriage coaches. In our work, we focus on members of the Army, Navy, Marine Corps, Air Force, and Coast Guard and their spouses. The tools and skills every married couple needs to thrive are the same, but the issues faced by military couples are often compounded by the unique challenges of military life, and we want to help as many of these couples as possible make it through those challenges together.

Creating a successful marriage is like navigating a minefield. Imagine being ordered to walk through a minefield on your own with no clue as to where the mines are buried. Not a very enticing proposition, is it? Every step you take is filled with a high degree of trepidation and fear. You don't know if or when you'll make a fatal mistake, causing a mine to go off and take you with it. Now imagine being faced with the same task, but this time, you have the help and mentorship of combat-tested guides who have successfully made it through that very same minefield. We are those guides. We're offering you a map to follow to create your own marital success. With this resource, you'll clearly see the mines and be able to avoid them. You'll have rock-solid confidence that you can succeed at what you once viewed as a high-risk mission.

Improvement and growth don't come without commitment, sacrifice, and effort in any area of life, and your marriage is no different. The information presented here can only make a positive change if at least one of you is willing to apply it. In each chapter, we share practical steps and exercises you can use right away. That's where the transformation happens, in taking action. If your lifemate isn't on board with this work yet, that's okay. Start by working on yourself.

As you read through this book, and especially if you find yourself stuck or confused about what to do next, we suggest you pray and meditate on the following questions and take action accordingly.

- *What do I need to do* to become a better man or woman?

- *What do I need to do* to become a better husband or wife, a better Christian (or Muslim, Jew, or Buddhist, etc.), and a better friend and partner to my lifemate?

- *What do I need to change* to become a better husband or wife, a better Christian (or Muslim, Jew, or Buddhist, etc.), and a better friend and partner to my lifemate?

- *What do I need to sacrifice or give up* to become a better husband or wife, a better Christian (or Muslim, Jew, or Buddhist, etc.), and a better friend and partner to my lifemate?

- *What commitments do I need to make or rededicate myself to* in order to become a better husband or wife, a better Christian (or Muslim, Jew, or Buddhist, etc.), and a better friend and partner to my lifemate?

If you and your lifemate have chosen to do this work together, you may also want to assemble a small group of friends or other likeminded couples interested in joining you. We encourage you to do so. Surrounding yourself with people who believe in the institution of marriage and support you in working on yours can only help. Building a strong, vibrant marriage takes work, and we pray that you'll commit to mastering the skills necessary to transform your marriage and elevate it to higher levels of passion, more effective communication, deeper intimacy, and a shared sense of purpose.

If you want better communication in your marriage, download our free gift to you, the Rules of Engagement Checklist for Effective Communication at lifem8z.com/communication-checklist. Don't wait until your marriage is under fire to begin. In peacetime, we prepare for war. The best time to make your marriage the best it can be is now.

CHAPTER 1

Know Your Mission and Commit to It

The room was spinning as I (Michael) dragged myself out of bed and made my way to the bathroom to pay homage to the porcelain god. When I finally got to my feet, I leaned over the sink to wash my face, and in that moment, I caught a glimpse of myself in the mirror. I looked that man in the eyes, and I didn't like what I saw. The image was so clear and so disappointing that I went from drunk to sober in an instant. In my own eyes, I saw the future. If I kept behaving the way I had that night, I'd lose my family. Some other man would be tucking my kids into bed. Some other man would be holding my wife, dancing with her, making love to the woman I loved.

Earlier that evening, my wife, Myra, and I had gone to a costume party, and I'd spent way too much time dancing with a woman in a skintight devil costume who had pulled me out onto the dance floor. Once again, I'd let my outgoing, gregarious nature turn into drinking too much and disrespecting my wife by giving my attention to another woman. I'd given no thought to how Myra must have felt as she sat in a corner and watched me carry on and cut up. It had been a long, quiet car ride home, and now, my pregnant wife lay curled up in bed, facing the wall so she wouldn't have to face me. She was turning away from me, and I couldn't blame her.

If I wanted to save my marriage, I had to take Michael Jackson's advice and start with the man in the mirror. My "work hard, play hard" lifestyle had to go. I had to put away those childish things if I really wanted Myra to be my life-mate—and I really did. I loved her. She was a wonderful wife, and she deserved a better husband. It was time for me to put her back on the pedestal I'd had her on when I was trying to win her affection. I'd created the problem, and it was up to me to fix it or face the prospect of losing her.

It's easy to have those kind of "I promise I'll never do that again" epiphanies under a haze of alcohol, looking back on the bad choices you've made in the night and dreading what you might have to face in the morning. But this was different. I couldn't have been clearer about where I'd gone wrong and everything I was putting at risk. I had to make a permanent change and show my wife she was the most important person in my life. I had to make sure she knew no amount of superficial fun mattered more than our relationship. I had to convince her *with my actions* that I would be different; our marriage would be different and better.

Up until that night, I hadn't been prepared to fully commit to the mission of marriage, but I'd reached a turning point. It would be an imperfect journey for me, marked by ups and downs, but I would see it through. When Myra and I married in 1980, I didn't fully understand the true mission of marriage. But over time, I learned it boils down to one thing. *The mission of marriage is to make sure your lifemate's needs are met.* If you don't, someone else just might.

ARE YOU READY TO COMMIT?

The decision to enter military service is serious business because you may be called upon to lay down your life for your nation. Marriage requires a very similar, deep commitment, and you can't complete your mission without it. When you decide to get married, you have to ask yourself if you're ready to dedicate your life to your spouse. (If you've already been married for a while, ask yourself if you're ready to recommit and rededicate your life to your spouse.) It's the only way to create a happy and fulfilling marriage for both of you.

To be honest, I really didn't think much about what it meant to dedicate my life to my country or to my lifemate, Myra, when I made those choices. As for military service, I was focused on being a part of a winning team. When I joined the Air Force, I initially viewed military service as a stepping stone and great resume material. As a college sophomore, majoring in psychology, I realized you can't do much with a psychology degree unless you earn a master's degree or a PhD. I wasn't sure I wanted to enroll in graduate school right after finishing my undergraduate studies, so I needed another option.

One day, early in my sophomore year of college, I was walking through campus with thoughts about my future bouncing around in my head. I had walked past the ROTC (Reserve Officers Training Corps) Detachment 585 building many times, but that day was different. Perhaps I was influenced by a subtle suggestion from my retired Chief Master Sergeant (CMSgt/E-9) father. It might have been by chance, but I'd like to think it was fate. Whatever the case, I decided to stop, walk in the door, and express my interest in becoming an Air Force officer. That decision changed my life.

One of the things that attracted me (Myra) to Michael was that he had traveled and had seen the world. Growing up in High Point, North Carolina, I'd always wanted to travel, so much so that I was entertaining thoughts of becoming a stewardess (now called flight attendants). Michael made his decision to join the AFROTC the year before I arrived on campus. It was fate (or God) that caused our lives to intersect at the right moment, in the right place. I knew Michael was going into the military, and all I could think was, "I'll finally get a chance to see the world." I looked forward to all the excitement being a military wife would bring.

When Michael announced his first assignment would be Great Falls, Montana, I thought, "Where is that?" When I imagined traveling, I had sunny vacation spots like Florida in mind. But I was raised to make the best of things, and I opened my mind to the possibilities and excitement that lay ahead. My first decision was to get excited about Great Falls. I had never heard of the town, so I looked it up on the map and reminded myself, "You've always prayed for an opportunity to travel. Well, here it is. Go for it. You'll be okay!" Going where the Air Force sent us was part of my commitment to my husband.

The decision to commit and to recommit—to the military and to your marriage—is one you'll have to make over and over again. It's one thing to say, "I'm thinking about becoming a Marine." It's quite another to walk into the Marine recruiter's office to sign up and take the oath. That's commitment in action. You know you'll be severely tested during boot camp. Deep down inside, you know you're about to undergo the most difficult challenge of your life. But you also know if all those other people made it through boot camp to be recognized as Marines, then you can too. When you begin in-processing, you physically and mentally prepare yourself to endure and overcome the challenges or threats that might confront you. That commitment to the military is life-changing, and you'd be wise to ask yourself, "Am I ready to commit?" before you make that choice.

I (Myra) asked myself the same question when Michael proposed to me. *Am I ready to commit to marriage?* Michael had made up his mind that he wanted to propose to me. He'd talked to his father, who told him, "Boy, you'd better marry that girl." Michael had also spoken with my father and asked for his blessing, which my father gave along with permission for Michael to fly me out to California to propose. From what he knew about marriage at that time, Michael believed he was ready for it.

Michael was completing his missile training at Vandenberg Air Force Base. When I arrived, we toured the California Central Coast towns of Lompoc, Santa Maria, San Luis Obispo, Solvang, and Santa Barbara. Each city was more beautiful than the last, but the beaches of Vandenberg Air Force Base captivated me. As we walked along the base's coastline, Michael pointed out the sea lions playing in the surf. We stopped to explore the tidal pools thriving with starfish, sea urchins, coral, and mussels, and I was enchanted by it all.

We'd been on the beach about an hour when Michael announced we needed to turn around because the tide was coming in and we didn't want our return route to be cut off. I could tell something was going on when he stopped and asked me to sit on a large rock. He got down on one knee— I was still wondering what was going on—and he asked me to marry him. He caught me completely by surprise. I didn't know how to answer him, so I just said, "I'll have to think about it." I wanted to be sure I was ready. But Michael later explained what my cautious, noncommittal response left him thinking. Because I was still in college, he figured I'd found another boyfriend.

Michael completed his initial technical training and transferred to Malmstrom Air Force Base in Great Falls, Montana. This was before email, Skype, and text messaging, but he called me every other day. We spent many hours (and a lot of money because we paid by the minute for those long-distance calls) talking on the phone and sometimes just listening to each other breathe. I missed him so much and soon made up my mind that he was "the one" and I was ready to marry him. I changed my answer to his proposal to a solid "yes."

No one can tell you if you're prepared for marriage or not. Like Michael, you might feel sure, or like Myra, you might need some time to think about it. Imagine a group of friends out for a bungee-jumping adventure. A few people will step up to jump without hesitation. Others will need a moment to assess the situation one last time before they take a deep breath and jump off the bridge. And then there's the final group. That group of people, experiencing intense fear, will struggle to take the plunge. The thing they all have in common is they do eventually jump. If you're trying to decide whether or not you're ready to commit to marriage, you have to do it in your own time and in your own way.

Whether you're considering cohabitation, a long-term relationship, or marriage, you must ask yourself if you're truly ready to commit to this person. This commitment goes deeper than the initial love and desire you feel for each other. Even if you're already married, you're not off the hook. There will be times when your love wanes and your desire seems like a distant memory. If you want your marriage to survive, you'll need to recommit to the mission.

When we ask the couples who come to us for marriage and relationship coaching and mentoring, "Do you love your partner?" practically all of them respond, "Yes!" However, when we ask them to define love, many struggle to find the words. Often, they describe love in terms of feelings. When we press them and ask what happens when your mate acts in unloving ways or is unwilling or unable to respond or return that love, they often indicate that would be a deal-breaker. We then share the following true story.

We were family friends with a couple who'd been married for more than fifty years. (To protect their privacy, we'll call her Grace and him Jacob.) Unfortunately, Jacob was stricken with Alzheimer's disease, a terrible illness that destroys memory and other important cognitive functions. Grace was a very petite woman, barely five feet tall; Jacob was nearly six feet tall. It wasn't easy, but as the disease progressed, Grace continued to care for Jacob alone at home. She sang hymns to him and read him Bible verses.

Over time, Jacob's personality changed drastically, and he lost the ability to recognize the most important people in his life, including his wife, Grace. (For those closest to the patient, this is often the most painful part of the disease.) Sometimes, as Grace tried to care for Jacob, he struggled with her, striking out at her or throwing things at her. Eventually, Jacob's behavior became so rough that Grace realized she could no longer care for her husband alone. She made the hard decision to have Jacob admitted to the Extended Care Center at the Veterans Medical Center. While Jacob was there, Grace continued to visit him, sing to him, and read to him every day. She did so for six long years until he eventually died.

Grace's love for Jacob shows us a powerful demonstration of unconditional, selfless love. She exhibited a depth of love and an understanding of the true mission of marriage that every couple should embrace. She upheld her wedding vows "to have and to hold, for better or for worse, in sickness and in health." Jacob was eventually incapable of acknowledging Grace's efforts or returning her acts of love in any way. Even so, she continued to pour her love, heart, and soul into her husband, expecting nothing in return. What an amazing act of love, commitment, and marriage.

Most Medal of Honor recipients don't consider themselves heroes. Instead, they say they simply did what they had to do. Grace would say the same about the way she cared for her husband. Before you marry, you should mentally prepare yourself for the possibility that your lifemate may get sick, injured, or debilitated, and you'll be faced with the decision to be their caretaker or break your commitment. None of us knows what the future holds, but we have to prepare ourselves to be ready to face life together, no matter what blessings and challenges we encounter.

Of course, marriage usually starts off on a better note. We love watching couples, often in the early stages of their relationship, who genuinely love one another. You can feel the heat of their passion all the way across the room. They can't take their eyes off each other. They hold each other's hands. They play footsies under the table. They may even kiss each other in public, and people watching may think or even tell them, "Get a room!" However, in time, many of those once-passionate relationships begin to fall apart. Don't think it can't happen to you. The best way to protect against it is to understand how and why these relationships devolve from bliss to white-hot hatred or bland disinterest.

WHY GOOD RELATIONSHIPS GO BAD

We're deeply disheartened when we see a husband and wife who used to love each other get to the point that they can't stand to be around each other. We know it doesn't have to be this way for any couple. Their marriage has somehow derailed, but how did it happen? Where did they go wrong? It doesn't happen overnight. It happens gradually, day by day. The underlying cause is simple. They lack commitment to the mission—sometimes because they don't know the mission, sometimes because they expected it to be easy to accomplish.

Commitment requires you to make the decision to be all in, to persevere and overcome any challenge you may face, no matter what. It requires you to accept the mission of marriage and do your very best to make sure your mate's needs are met even when it's difficult or you don't feel like it. Commitment says, "I will not fail." You may encounter conflict, but you work hard to resolve it. You may face issues of broken trust, but you can choose to work through it and navigate your relationship back to a place of trust and security. Marriage isn't easy, but if you commit to doing the work, it can be one of the most rewarding and enriching experiences of your life. Without that commitment, the marriage cannot thrive and may not survive.

HOW MUCH DO YOU VALUE YOUR LIFEMATE?

Your level of commitment is a reflection of how much you value the person you've chosen as a lifemate. So how much do you value your spouse? Your instinct might be to say, "More than anything," but first, to really understand this question, we have to go back to the beginning. We have to examine the nature of the very first relationship between a man and a woman. At the start of most of our couple's coaching and mentoring sessions, we ask: "When was the first time God said, 'It is not good'?" We smile as we watch each couple struggle to provide the right answer. They often say, "Was it when Adam and Eve ate the forbidden fruit?" No. "Was it when they listened to the serpent?" No. "Was it when they disobeyed God?" Again, we say no. After we allow them to struggle for a few minutes, we jump in to rescue them with the answer.

We recount the Creation story, as captured in the first and second chapters of Genesis, in the Old Testament of the Bible. As God created the heavens and the earth, He created light and separated the waters from the land, and He created seed-bearing plants and fruit-bearing trees and set the lights in the sky to separate light from darkness, and He created animals both male and female, and He created man in His own image. After each of these miraculous events, God said, "It is good." However, late in chapter two, God notices that Adam is alone.

Now, we don't believe God makes mistakes. Consider the possibility that God created Adam and allowed him to be alone to emphasize a point and stage a crucial message for us. God made all the other animals male and female but strayed from this approach with Adam. It wasn't until the very end of the second chapter of Genesis that God said, "It is not good for the man to be alone. I will make a helper suitable for him" Genesis 2:18 (NIV). So God caused the man to fall into a deep sleep, and while the man slept, God created woman, and He brought her to Adam, and Adam exclaimed, "At last! She is bone from my bone and flesh from my flesh!"

God recognized that it wasn't good for Adam to be alone, so He made Adam a companion. In essence, *woman is God's gift to man*, and every man should see his wife that way. While the Bible doesn't explicitly say that a wife should see her husband as a gift too, we believe it's safe to make that leap. 1 Corinthians 7:4 (NIV) says, "The wife does not have authority over her own body but yields it to her husband. In the same way, the husband does not have authority over his own body but yields it to his wife." You belong to each other, and you should value each other equally.

Do you see your spouse as a gift to you? If not (as you search your heart and answer honestly), did you highly value your lifemate when you first met and fell in love? Now men, if God were to separate the clouds and cause a brilliant beam of heavenly light to appear, and through that light God presented a beautiful artifact and placed it in your hands, and you heard God's thundering voice say to you, "This is my gift to you," how would you treat that gift? Think about it. Would you cherish it? Would you set it in a place of honor and reverence? Would you protect it? Would you want to let the whole world know God chose you and honored you, above all other men, with this gift with value beyond measure? That's exactly the image you, as a man, should have of your wife. Your wife is God's gift to you.

That first relationship, between Adam and Eve, established the foundation for every male-female relationship to follow. So let's explore how solid your foundation is. If God were to stop by to check up on you, what would He see? Would He see you taking good care of your gift and celebrating the great honor He has bestowed on you? Would He see you actively pursuing your marriage mission of making sure your spouse's needs are met? Or would God find that you've demoted His gift from the mantel, where it once occupied a place of honor, to a dusty, web-covered box in the attic? If you're not one hundred percent happy with your responses to these questions and you want to change, we can tell you how. It is possible to get back to the place where you were so excited by your lifemate that you could barely go a day, an hour, or a minute without seeing her, talking to him, holding her, and smelling him. Overcoming complacency is the key.

DEFEND AGAINST THE THREAT OF COMPLACENCY

We used to believe a lack of communication was the number one cause of divorce and broken relationships, but recently, we've taken that a little further. In our work with hundreds of couples, we've found that a failure to communicate isn't the greatest threat to your marriage. *The number one threat to any marriage is complacency.* We communicate very well when we're courting each other, but as the relationship becomes familiar, we become complacent. Complacency is a clear and present danger that threatens to attack, infect, and destroy the delicate fabric of love, passion, intimacy, and commitment. When complacency sets in, communication is no longer a priority. Yes, the lack of communication is a problem, but at the root of that problem is complacency. In fact, we haven't seen one marriage issue that couldn't be traced back to the insidious presence of complacency in one or both partners.

Men love the thrill of the hunt. They love the art and mystery of the pursuit. When a man is dating (or chasing) a woman he wants to be with and get to know better, he pulls out all the stops to show how much he values her and what a great guy he is. He showers twice a day and keeps his car washed and waxed so he can impress her. He listens when she talks and helps in the kitchen. But once a man believes he has the woman, things tend to change. In the early phases of falling in love, a man captures a woman's attention by persistently pursuing and wooing her. After he says, "I do," he stops doing those things. He stops opening doors for her (if he ever did). He forgets to tell her how beautiful she is. Instead of listening to her talk about her day, he comes home, forgets to kiss her hello, and drops in his chair with the remote in one hand and a Michelob in the other. "Honey, bring me another beer" is as much of a conversation as he can muster.

When a man is pursuing her, the endorphin rush from the chase motivates the woman to look her best. If she feels her new love interest likes a certain hairstyle, she'll wear it for him. If he's communicated (verbally or nonverbally) that he likes a particular perfume, she'll be sure to wear it. Over time though, the woman stops doing the things that inspired him to pursue her with passion and, ultimately, won him over. She falls into a routine focused on work, home, and the kids. The days of dressing up to go out with him and making sure he left the house with her on his mind every morning are gone.

Early on in most relationships, each partner viewed the other as an amazing gift to be cherished, honored, protected, and revered. The critical error most men and women make: we gradually begin to take each other for granted, and day by day, we become more and more complacent. During the tens of thousands of hours we've spent coaching and mentoring couples, we've observed the insidious nature of complacency. When not addressed, complacency hinders the growth and health of the relationship, and ultimately, the relationship will die.

The bottom line is that complacency is at the root of all the marriage problems our clients and workshop attendees complain about. It's the reason for arguments, secrets and lies, and the silent treatment. Complacency is even at the root of adultery. When you see your mate as a gift and you're committed to the mission, you protect your marriage from complacency, but you have to stay vigilant. Complacency is a stealthy enemy. It starts small and grows over time. It chips away at your marriage, little by little, until you're left wondering where the love went and why you're married to this person. It's a slow erosion, and by the time you notice the damage, it may seem like it's too late to save your marriage.

Couples experiencing the bliss of young love are completely in tune to each other. You've probably heard the saying, "What you did to catch him or her, you have to continue to do to keep him or her." That saying is true, but few of us live by it after we say, "I do." We get comfortable and start to take our lifemate for granted, and the relationship changes. Most of the time, we're unaware of the gradual changes taking place in our relationship. Instead of cuddling on the couch to watch TV together, we sit in separate chairs or in separate rooms. Instead of kissing passionately, our kisses dwindle to mere pecks on the cheek or air-blown kisses.

The good news is that, while we can't fix everything, we can fix anything we focus on. Be aware that your lifemate continues to need to feel loved by you after you're married. Ask your lifemate what you can do to make him or her feel loved and be consistent in providing it. Don't let complacency sneak in and destroy your marriage.

THE BENEFITS AND CHALLENGES OF MILITARY LIFE

In our marriage coaching and mentorship, we share fundamental marriage skills that apply to any serious, committed relationship. However, military life adds a layer of complexity that other marriages won't face. The women and men who answer the call to serve this great nation by joining the military are unique. Their decision to serve places them among the ranks of other citizen-soldiers choosing to potentially sacrifice their all for the purpose of freedom. While this book focuses on overcoming the challenges military couples face, we want to emphasize that the pros of military life far outweigh the cons. Here are just a few of the positive benefits military life provides:

- Great pay and path for advancement
- Professional, leadership, and personal development
- Travel across the nation and around the world
- A strong culture of wellness and physical fitness

- World-class fitness, bowling, swimming, and recreation centers
- Full medical, vision, dental, and prescription coverage for military members and their families (for life if you serve a full career)
- Free legal services
- Discounted groceries, clothing, electronic entertainment, and childcare
- Discounted vacation resorts at Disney, in Hawaii, and some international venues
- Opportunities to work alongside and meet people from other ethnic groups and cultures
- Outstanding retirement benefits
- An immense sense of pride in wearing the uniform and intense satisfaction from what you do

The list goes on and on. While the benefits of military life can't be denied, you can't afford to ignore the challenges that come as part of the package. Few people outside of military life can fully comprehend the unique challenges we face and how those challenges can affect us, our families, and our marriages. The inherent dangers of military life combined with concerns about the potential or actual consequences of our profession can create a lot of pressure on service members and their families. Because of this, military members under stress may sometimes pull away from their families, especially as they get closer to and begin preparing for deployment and combat. Many cope with the high level of pressure by trying to escape from thoughts about the potential dangers they may face.

Our best advice for the spouse of a military member who is pulling away as they spin-up for deployment: *don't pursue*. Of course, you want to be there to connect to your spouse and help him or her through this process. Just let your husband or wife know you're there to listen, but give your spouse the needed space to prepare for that upcoming deployment and to do everything possible to return safely. (Deployment is an important issue, and we address it at greater length in chapter six.)

Frequent moves can also be a blessing or a curse for military families. Relocating every two or three years is one of the realities of military life. For some, the moves generate a lot of havoc and upheaval. Spouses quit yet another job to follow their military partner again; parents rip children from their circle of friends and their school; the entire family leaves a familiar community for a new one. Family members look at what they're being asked to give up, and they may feel some regret or resentment.

From the outside, moving just as your family has started to settle into a place can seem like a no-win situation, but many families see it differently. They treat relocating as a benefit of military life, and so for them, the moves provide a sense of adventure and opportunity. These families look forward to discovering new places, forming new friendships, and having new experiences. They're excited to see where life in the military will take them. The moves are an opportunity to pursue adventures, to explore other cultures, and to see the world. Frequent moves are a reality of military life.

The sooner you embrace this fact, the better off you and your family will be. One of the biggest mistakes a military dependent spouse can make is to decide they don't want to travel when their military sponsor is assigned to a new duty station. Marriage by itself is hard, but the complexity is compounded when you decide to have a long-distance marriage. Doing so opens the door to infidelity and possibly divorce. The most successful military couples make the best of each move, looking forward to the chance to make new friends and teaching their children to do the same. Concerned parents tend to worry a lot about how the moves affect their children. In most cases, children take their cues from their parents, and military brats (a term we military dependents proudly embrace) adapt very well to the changes associated with change of station moves.

As a couple, you should handle the moving details together as much as possible, knowing there will be times when one spouse may have to handle everything alone because the military member has to leave early. During our Air Force career, we had at least two moves for which Myra had to handle all the details by herself because I (Michael) had been called away to report early to the duty assignment. I knew this would be a big deal for her, and I saw how it could have easily escalated into an incredible stressor for Myra, me, our children, and our marriage.

In the past, we had always moved together, so the first time Michael told me (Myra) that he had to leave for his assignment and I'd have to manage the move on my own, I was nervous. I was used to supervising the kids and keeping them out of the way while Michael dealt with the movers and handled the details. I couldn't imagine how I'd handle the move and manage the kids, a second-grader and a third-grader, all by myself. Michael reminded me that I already knew everything I needed to do, but I also had to do some serious self-talk and encourage myself. I had a conversation with our daughters, Lindsay and Lauren, and let them know they'd both have to work with me to make this happen. I think they saw the fear in my eyes and decided they wanted to help me, and they did.

Whenever I started to worry about the move, I reminded myself that Michael hadn't chosen this for us. The job required him to leave right away, and it wasn't his fault that I was left with all the responsibility. Our other moves had happened during the summer, but this time, Michael left in January, and we agreed it was best to let the girls finish out their school year where they'd started it. Taking all of that into consideration, I realized we didn't have many options. I committed to getting the job done, and in the end, the details of the move fell into place. In the process, I realized I can do hard things by myself, and I learned that my girls would listen and obey when I needed them to. In fact, they turned out to be great little helpers. Lindsay, our older child, who'd had great people skills from a very young age, even stepped up as a little leader and supervised her younger sister.

When you're in the thick of it, remember the move is the villain, not either one of you. A positive attitude will do a lot to help you through trying times like these. If you find yourself slipping into complaining, resentment, or measuring whether or not your mate does as much for the family as you do, remember the mission. Your role is to make sure your spouse's needs are met. Focus on that.

Michael was fortunate to be the son of a Non-Commissioned Officer (NCO). He had traveled the world as a military brat. I (Myra), on the other hand, had always wanted to travel but grew up never having left my home state of North Carolina. Early on, Michael told me he'd never had a bad assignment growing up, and I held on to that reassuring thought as we made each move. As our plane began its approach into Great Falls, where we had our first assignment, I asked Michael, "What's that white stuff on the ground?" He responded, "Oh, that's snow." It was the first of June!

While it was completely different from where I'd grown up, we enjoyed the small town, northwestern feel. We spent several weekends exploring Helena and the Gates of the Mountains, discovered by Lewis and Clark and located halfway between Yellowstone and Glacier National Parks. We made the most of everything the area had to offer. From that first assignment until our last, I was able to make the most of every place we lived.

A friend of ours, whose husband was in the Air Force and whose assignments paralleled ours, had a very different experience in Great Falls, Montana. She hated it. After Montana, we got stationed at Vandenberg Air Force base in California, an hour north of Santa Barbara, an hour south of San Luis Obispo, and three hours north of Los Angeles. We loved it. We got out there and enjoyed the oceans. We took advantage of the restaurants, the tourist attractions, and the Southern California lifestyle. Our friend was also stationed there, and once again, his wife hated it. Later, we got stationed in Omaha, Nebraska, together. Initially, I wasn't that excited about the assignment, but once we got settled in, we discovered Omaha's music scene, and we had a fantastic time. Our friend's wife, well, once again, she hated it.

No matter where they were stationed, she was unhappy. Finally, we all made our way back to the East Coast. We were stationed in Hampton, Virginia, and they were eventually stationed in Northern Virginia. Even then, she was dissatisfied. She spent more than twenty years of her life unhappy with where she was "forced" to live. For more than two decades, we lived in most of the same places. While she suffered, we thrived. The only difference between her experience and ours was the attitude we each brought to it.

One day, our daughter Lauren came home from school and shared a quote she had learned. "Daddy," she said, "attitude is the paintbrush of the mind." When your family is making a move, you get to decide how you'll paint the situation. If you have a positive attitude, you recognize that the choice is yours. You can decide that, instead of being down, you'll choose to be up because up is definitely better. The move is happening. You get to decide whether or not you'll enjoy your new home.

A high-stress job, like a career in the military, doesn't have to equal a high-stress marriage, but it's important for the military member to find the best possible balance between work and home life. When Michael first went into the military, he was quickly identified as a fast burner, one to watch for leadership and strong promotion potential. He started associating with the guys who were really making things happen at the missile wing. They didn't just put in eight hours a day. They put in ten to twelve hours a day, and it was considered a badge of honor to sometimes work up to fourteen or even sixteen hours. They wanted to be the best, and they were proud of being recognized as such. They took extreme pride in their work ethic, constantly striving to out-produce and out-perform any other member of the unit.

I knew Michael worked in a high-pressure job. I listened attentively when he described the extremely high performance standards they operated under. I understood because he was responsible for nuclear weapons and there was no room for error. But that "work hard" mentality had an ugly side. Michael and his Air Force buddies also partied extremely hard. There was no balance. They were in the clubs up to four nights a week. It took a huge toll on the wives and families, and some of the women reached their breaking point.

One young wife walked into the Officer's Club bar, pushing her baby in a stroller. She marched up to her husband and said, "It's not fair that you spend all your time here and I have to watch the kids." She shoved the stroller and baby at him. "Here. Take it," she told her husband while we all looked on. While I was never pushed to that limit, I did notice that the guys—including my guy—didn't pay much attention to their spouses. Instead, they huddled together, talking about work, leaving the women sitting over in the corner, left out and feeling alone and abandoned.

Yes, one of you has chosen a stressful profession, and the other of you has agreed to support that person in that choice, but you still have to prioritize your relationship. There will be challenges along the way, but you can choose to fight for your marriage. Be aware of the fact that you have an added element of stress in your lives, but don't let it derail your relationship. Don't let your high-stress profession create a high-stress marriage. Remember the mission—to make sure your lifemate's needs are met—and use the tools we share here to fulfill that mission.

BEFORE YOU BLAME YOUR MATE, FIRST EXAMINE YOURSELF

If you've read this far, then you've noticed we don't spend any time telling you how you can change your mate. Early in our marriage, when Michael was exhibiting those behaviors that left me feeling disrespected and alone, I (Myra) made a decision. I was committed to our marriage. My religious upbringing emphasized the importance of marriage, and I took that seriously. However, I also knew I wasn't going to change Michael by nagging him. I would've been within my rights to complain and demand that he change, but I didn't want to fall into that trap. Nagging would have pushed him away instead of bringing him back to me.

Instead, I remembered how good our relationship had been in the courting phase, and I held on to those memories. Rather than focusing on how Michael needed to change, I focused on me. I made it a point to be there for him in whatever ways I could. I did special things for him and made it clear that I wanted to spend time with him. I cooked his favorite dinners and sat close to him when we were watching TV. Even if I didn't feel like going out, if he wanted to go, I went with him.

My husband later explained that my loving treatment of him became a mirror that reflected back to him his unloving treatment of me. He finally saw the pain he was inflicting on me, and because he loved me, he decided to change. Because we each focused on becoming the best lifemate we could be, our marriage survived those stressful times and came out better than it had been in the beginning.

As we mentioned earlier, we believe every man and woman in a relationship needs to regularly ask themselves the following questions:

- *What do I need to do* to become a better man or woman?

- *What do I need to do* to become a better husband or wife, a better Christian (or Muslim, Jew, or Buddhist, etc.), and a better friend and partner to my lifemate?

- *What do I need to change* to become a better husband or wife, a better Christian (or Muslim, Jew, or Buddhist, etc.), and a better friend and partner to my lifemate?

- *What do I need to sacrifice or give up* to become a better husband or wife, a better Christian (or Muslim, Jew, or Buddhist, etc.), and a better friend and partner to my lifemate?

- *What commitments do I need to make or rededicate myself* to in order to become a better husband or wife, a better Christian (or Muslim, Jew, or Buddhist, etc.), and a better friend and partner to my lifemate?

Instead of making New Year's resolutions to read more, watch less television, or get in better shape, use these questions to challenge yourself to grow as a man or a woman, a husband or a wife, and a friend to your lifemate. You don't have to wait until next year rolls around to resolve to do better. Start to identify your self-improvement areas today. Then, set specific goals for those areas and develop action plans focused on the steps you need to take to achieve those goals.

In each area, assess:

1. Where you are
2. Where you want to be
3. What you need to do to get there
4. Your progress and success

During our time in the military and in our life since retirement, we've seen too many marriages in crisis, couples who love one another but don't know how to show it. There's no need to live a life of silent desperation. We've worked with couples who've struggled in their marriage for years and come to us seeking healing and hope. Many of those couples have tried everything—counseling, therapy, and support groups—to no avail. They come to us to give their marriage one last shot before divorce. They come expecting very little since everything else has failed, but those who do the work leave more deeply in love and committed to each other.

Know the mission of your marriage and commit to it. Be willing to do what it takes to make sure your lifemate's needs are met. Your successful military marriage starts with you.

Create Your LifeM8Z Moment

Think about your responses to each question or prompt individually, and then turn to each other and thoughtfully share your responses.

1. In what ways are you ready to commit to a long-term relationship?

2. If you're not married yet, are there any areas of your life that you need to work on before you commit to marriage?

3. If you are married, what have you done (or what do you need to do) to strengthen your lifelong commitment to your marriage?

4a. (Men) In what ways do you see your lifemate as a gift from God? How do you show her you see her as a gift?

4b. (Ladies) In what ways do you see your life-mate as a gift from God? How do you show him you see him as a gift?

5. What preventive actions are you going to take to ensure complacency doesn't creep in and damage your relationship?

CHAPTER 2

Get What You Want by Giving What Your Lifemate Needs

When Robert and Kelly[1], both members of the military, came to us for marriage coaching, it didn't take long to figure out what had gone wrong in their relationship. Kelly was a quintessential strong black woman, and she exuded that strength in the way she carried herself. The pride she took in her appearance was obvious, and she clearly articulated her vision for the future. Robert, on the other hand, was a bit of a slob and lacked the necessary motivation to build a secure future for his family. While his wife was a presence in the room, he faded into the background.

We did our best to help Kelly and Robert reconnect, but Robert had no real interest in changing his behavior. He showed up for their coaching sessions, probably to appease his wife, but back at home, he chose not to apply what they'd learned. Eventually, the couple divorced, and Kelly invested her time and energy in healing from that failed relationship and falling back in love with herself. The next time we saw

---

1 Names and identifying details of our clients have been changed to protect their privacy.

her professionally, Kelly came to us for pre-marriage coaching with the new man in her life. Wayne was also a service member, but the couple was much better matched than Kelly and Robert had been. Wayne and Kelly enjoyed spending their free time together. They talked openly and honestly and partnered on financial decisions and goals. They had a shared vision, and they were working together to bring that vision to life. Kelly finally had her emotional needs met in marriage, and she was equally invested in meeting Wayne's needs.

In Acts 20:35 (NIV), Paul reminds us that Jesus said, "It is more blessed to give than to receive," but God created us as selfish creatures. From birth, we cry when we want to eat, want to be changed, want to be held, or want to be driven around the block so we can go to sleep. Deep down inside, each of us believes the whole world revolves around us. It's our nature to think "I, me, and my" instead of "we, us, and our." Couples who fail to make the shift from "I" to "we" will struggle to discover the promises of love, joy, peace, patience, kindness, goodness, faithfulness, gentleness, and self-control (the fruit of the Spirit as found in Galatians 5:22-23) that a healthy marriage can yield.

The mission of marriage—*to meet your lifemate's needs*—requires the two of you to create an interdependent lifestyle. This doesn't mean your worlds completely revolve around each other. You each have work, friends, and interests you don't necessarily share, but you should also share a common set of friends and interests. You are in a relationship, which means you should be *relating* to on another. While it's okay to have separate friends and interests, your marriage should be the primary place where your most significant emotional needs are satisfied. The only legitimate place to seek that kind of fulfillment is within your marriage. In order to meet each other's needs, you have to understand what they are and be willing to do what it takes to fulfill them, even when doing so requires you to change.

You cannot wait for your lifemate to meet your needs first. Someone has to step up. Someone has to take the higher position, as Myra did early in our marriage. When I (Michael) wasn't meeting some of her emotional needs, my wife continued to show up and meet mine. Eventually, it hit home for me that I wanted to give her what she was giving me. If your marriage isn't in the best place at the moment, now more than ever you need to do what you can to make sure your spouse's needs are met.

Getting what you need by meeting your lifemate's needs is like priming a water pump. You can't just walk up to the pump and expect water to flow. You have to pour a little water in the top and then work the pump. The water and the pumping action work together to create a suction that gets the water to flow from the well. By continuing to meet my needs, Myra was priming the pump, and eventually, water flowed for her. Seeing the results of meeting your lifemate's needs may require patience, but it's worth it. It may take weeks, months, or sometimes even years, but in most cases, your spouse will recognize your efforts and respond in kind. Zig Ziglar said, "You can have everything in life that you want if you will just help other people get what they want." It's true in almost any relationship that you get out of it what you put into it, and it's certainly true in marriage.

Building a strong marriage requires hard work. It's an ongoing process. In 2019, as we write this book and celebrate our thirty-ninth wedding anniversary, we're still working on our relationship. And as long as we have breath in our bodies, we'll continue to work to make our marriage the best it can be by constantly striving to be the best lifemates we can be. We'll continue to work to meet each other's needs because we know it can mean the difference between a long and happy marriage and a stale or miserable existence endured in silent desperation or even ending in divorce. Make strengthening your marriage a lifelong adventure of discovering and meeting your lifemate's needs. Become an elite crusader in mastering the discipline of understanding, anticipating, and fulfilling those needs.

THE TOP 10 EMOTIONAL NEEDS

Human beings are hotwired to be self-seeking in our quest to fulfill our basic needs. We seek out food, water, shelter, and sex, among other things, to satisfy our physical needs. However, we also have basic emotional needs that need to be met, and these aren't always as easy to articulate, unless and until we're taught what they are. While we all have the same emotional needs, the way each person prioritizes them can vary greatly. However, during our seminars and coaching sessions, we ask men and women to rank their top five needs out of the ten we've adapted from *His Needs, Her Needs* (Revell, 2011) by Willard F. Harley, PhD, founder of Marriage Builders. In our experience, the gender breakdown is fairly consistent.

Five Basic Needs of Men	Five Basic Needs of Women
1. Sexual fulfillment	1. Affection and demonstrations of love
2. Recreational companionship	2. Intimate conversation
3. An attractive spouse	3. Honesty and openness
4. Domestic support	4. Financial support and partnership
5. Admiration and respect	5. Family commitment

Among our students, clients, and audiences, the top five needs of the men tend to be the women's bottom five, and the women's top five needs tend to rank as the bottom five for the men. Obviously, there are exceptions to this breakdown, but it's additional evidence that God has an amazing sense of humor. The only way to know how your lifemate ranks these needs is for the two of you to have a conversation about it. Sit down together, rank your top five needs, and share your lists with each other. Be open to the idea that what's most important for you may not even make the top five for your spouse. That's okay. What matters most is that you're each willing to respect the other's priorities and to do your best to become the source that fulfills those needs.

Notice that happiness isn't a need that makes those lists. That's because when you both find a way to fulfill these basic emotional needs for each other, happiness is a natural by-product. It would be unusual to find someone who has all of those needs met and still isn't happy.

As much as we'd like to believe it to be so, getting married doesn't mean your spouse can read your mind, so the next step is to ask your mate to provide five examples of how they would like you to meet each of their top five needs. As you do this and begin the process of becoming more intentional about meeting each other's needs, you will find yourselves becoming best friends and forging a formidable marriage.

It's fascinating how men and women so often prioritize their needs differently. Many men want sexual fulfillment first, while their wives are looking for affection. (Of course, the way you show your love and affection should reflect how your lifemate wants to be loved.) The need for sex by one spouse and intimacy by the other can create conflict in the marriage, especially since many men have learned to equate intimacy and affection with sex. When a woman asks for more intimacy, her husband may hear her saying, "More sex, please!" However, women typically seek intimacy by connecting through conversation first, and they have a genuine need for men to share and affirm their experiences, thoughts, and feelings.

Sometimes, it can be tough for men to find the right words to connect with their lifemates. As a general rule, men just aren't that big on expressing their feelings or sharing their deep thoughts, but women want men to be more expressive with them. It's one of the ways women connect, and it's important that men make the effort to meet this important need. I (Michael) sometimes struggle to keep up with Myra when we talk because she can easily jump from subject to subject. I watch in amazement as she and our daughters engage in conversational gymnastics when they talk, and they all easily flow with the conversation. It just doesn't come naturally to me, but I've learned to sit and listen anyway. It's important to my wife, and I want to fill that need for her. Men, you can go a long way towards fulfilling your wife's desire for conversation by simply answering questions like "How was your day?" with more than one-syllable answers or grunts and by actively listening while maintaining eye contact and holding her hand when your wife talks to you about whatever she has on her mind.

Of course, the need for sexual fulfillment should also be met in the marriage. The two of you may be on completely different pages about what this means, so it merits discussion. Sex is something most of us like to have, but it's a subject most couples never discuss. When we first married, I (Michael) thought that meant we were going to practice our "marriage ministry" all the time. I figured we'd have playtime in the morning before I left for work, again when I came home for lunch, and at least once again at night. I thought I was an amazing "stud muffin," but one day I sensed a need to ask Myra how she was enjoying our playtime sessions. To my despair, she responded, "Not so much." So I asked her what I could do to help her enjoy it as much as I did. I learned it was just too much for her. I needed to take into consideration that meeting my own needs should never come at the cost of leaving her worn out or hurt in any way. Talk with each other about how you can make sure you're both fulfilled sexually without causing any undue stress. It's one of the most important conversations you can have.

While many men really want a wife they can hang out and enjoy fun activities with, many women are more concerned with family commitment. They want to know their husband will be there for them. If they have children, women want to feel confident that their husband will be a strong presence for those children. They want to know he'll provide materially but also show up for games, recitals, and daddy-daughter dances. They want a partner in parenting and in creating and caring for a family.

Financial support and partnership are the sources of major disagreements in many marriages. (Many experts cite money issues as the number one cause of divorce. While we believe complacency is the number one cause of failed marriages, we do recognize that financial issues are a frequent contributor to marital strife.) Today, most couples have dual-income households. And in some cases, the woman earns more money than the man. When you shift your money conversations from "I, me, and my," to "we, us, and our," it no longer matters who makes more. It requires a certain level of trust, but at some point, you need to figure out how to pool your resources to accomplish your respective and common goals. You can attack debt and acquire wealth more rapidly when you work as a team. True financial partnership also means you avoid financial infidelity. Keeping secrets about the money you have coming in or going out can only damage the trust you're working to build. Choose to be fully transparent about your finances.

While most homes are dual-income, women still carry more of the housework and childcare load. At the end of the day, whether there's a stay-at-home parent involved or both spouses work outside of the home, no one person can be fully responsible for everything it takes to make your home your sanctuary. It's important to come up with a plan to fairly divide domestic responsibilities. A woman who gets married becomes a wife, not a cook or a maid. It's not reasonable to expect her to work eight hours a day and then come home and clean toilets, cook dinner, and take care of the kids all by herself. Some couples realize they need to sort out who'll handle what, but few connect these discussions back to the importance of meeting each other's fundamental emotional needs. It's crucial to the success of your marriage that you do.

ASK FOR WHAT YOU NEED: A TOOL YOU CAN USE

Your lifemate might think he or she is doing everything possible to meet your emotional needs. However, if you have a need that's going unmet, it's your responsibility to communicate that. Your spouse cannot read your mind. This can be particularly challenging for men because they tend to communicate on a single frequency. That frequency behaves much like a sonar beep. Beep: *I'm hungry.* Beep: *I want sex.* Beep: *I'm done talking.* Men say what they mean, and they are reluctant to share much of anything else that might be going on below the surface.

Women have a much more intricate and nuanced manner of communicating and often communicate indirectly. The communication style of women is much like a complex waveform. To completely understand women, you have to listen not only to the words, but also the emotion behind the words, along with the tone, body language, and facial expression. It also helps if you have some situational awareness of other loosely related issues. Neither style is better or worse than the other, but the danger is that men, who are used to plain, matter-of-fact talk, may miss the point of what women are saying. And women can cause their husbands to retreat internally with persistent attempts to get a deeper, more meaningful response from them.

You can't expect your spouse to guess what you need. You owe it to your lifemate, yourself, and your marriage to speak up when your needs are going unmet. Failing to speak up deprives your lifemate of a valuable opportunity to change and grow. This can sound intimidating, but when you apply the right tools, asking for what you need is easy. When you share what you need with each other, you actually give each other a precious gift. You're saying, "These are my needs and I trust you to fulfill them." When you're willing to hear that from your lifemate without judgment and do your best to affirm and meet those needs, you demonstrate that you're deserving of that trust.

The one tool we give to every couple we work with, even those who only have a single consultation with us, is the hand-in-hand, eye-to-eye, knee-to-knee communication process developed by Dr. David and Vera Mace, founders of Better Marriages (formerly known as the Association for Couples in Marriage Enrichment). Here's how it works. Sit comfortably, face your partner, knee-to-knee, and hold each other's hands. Look into each other's eyes, not just at each other's faces, because the eyes really are the windows to the soul. When was the last time you really saw each other? How long has it been since you gazed into your lifemate's eyes? How long has it been since you connected like this? Make that connection now.

Resist the temptation to avert your eyes. At first, you may giggle a little, and you may squirm a bit, but that's okay. Many couples initially comment, "All of this feels weird." But we encourage them to be patient and stay in the position. Sometimes, one or both parties sheds a tear because they haven't made time to sit down and to really connect with each other, looking at each other in this way, in a very long time. In this moment, you're not just gazing at your lifemate's face. You're looking at the person inside, the soul that's joined to yours through this journey of life. No matter what's going on in your relationship right now, that person you first kissed is still in there. That person you first made love to is still in there. That person you vowed to love and cherish for the rest of your life is still there. This is the only person in the world you can connect with in this way, on this level. This intimacy is reserved for your lifemate.

In this moment, in all the world, the only two people who matter are the two of you. As you sit quietly, hand-in-hand, eye-to-eye, knee-to-knee, you might actually feel your mate's heartbeat. Once you've settled down, affirm your love for each other. Share something positive with each other, and then discuss the issue or conflict you're experiencing, keeping the issue the main point of the discussion. Finally, share something positive, and then reaffirm your marriage.

When we use this tool with couples, more often than not, one or both of them tears up. We see two hundred pound men, who haven't shed a tear since they were little boys, weep as they look into their wife's eyes. Many couples tell us they can't remember ever being so present for each other or that they haven't looked into each other's eyes since their dating days. When you and your lifemate are both willing to participate in this process, you'll find it has the power to transform your marriage from miserable to masterful, from mediocre to marvelous.

This hand-in-hand, eye-to-eye, knee-to-knee posture creates a safe, trusting atmosphere for couples to communicate, to connect, to be understood, to understand, and to see feelings, issues, and experiences from their mate's perspective.

They can share the highs and lows of the day. They can express any concerns they have about themselves or their relationship. They can safely share when they feel their mate has disappointed, hurt, or angered them, and amazingly, they can share these things without any fear of emotions getting out of control. We encourage you to try it. The more you practice this communication technique, the better you will get at it.

IF YOU FAIL TO MEET YOUR LIFEMATE'S NEEDS

We'd been married for more than two decades, so I (Michael) thought I knew my wife pretty well. Maybe I did know Myra well, but I didn't know as much about women as I thought I did. The miseducation of Michael Holmes started when I was a kid growing up in the seventies. Guys talked a lot about Spanish Fly back then, and they always described it as making a woman "hot" so she wanted to have sex. Somehow, I conflated this idea with the idea of hot flashes. So after twenty-five years of marriage, I was looking forward to Myra entering menopause. The first time her "private summer" hit, we were in bed, and I was sure the hot flash was a signal of elevated sexual arousal.

As I felt my wife's body temperature spike, I thought, "She's ready. Go for it!" I rolled over, excited about the playtime to come, and wrapped my arms around her. Instead of giving me a warm welcome, Myra yelled, "Get off me!

Get off me!" and struggled to get away. I'd completely mis-read her signals. I would've done better by turning on a fan. (Men, I hope I've saved some of you from making the same mistake.) Myra and I look back on that misunderstanding and laugh because I was so far off in interpreting her needs. It was a minor blip in our relationship, but sometimes mis-understanding your lifemate's needs can lead to more serious problems when it means those needs go unfulfilled.

Unmet needs create vulnerabilities in a marriage. They open the door for other people (or other things) to interfere in your marriage. Here's what we mean. Let's say Myra stops making lunch for me (Michael) when we're home together even though that's our routine. One afternoon, I go walk-ing down the street, and our neighbor, Ms. X, sees me walk-ing by and says, "Hey, Michael. I just made these delicious sandwiches with potato salad and fresh-squeezed lemonade. Would you like to come in for lunch?" My stomach is growl-ing, and her lunch sounds tempting. In that moment, I have to make a decision. Do I go in and eat lunch in some other lady's kitchen, or do I keep walking? If my wife had met my need for lunch, I could just say, "No, thanks. I just enjoyed lunch with my wife," without giving it a second thought.

That example is an oversimplification, of course, but it's also right on the mark. As human beings, we have a strong desire to have our emotional needs met and we ac-tively (or unconsciously) seek out ways to make it happen. If your needs go unmet at home, you're likely to try to find fulfillment elsewhere. If a husband never wants to share his feelings with his wife, he leaves his marriage vulnerable to a man who's more than willing to pour his heart out to her. If a wife withholds sex from her husband, she increases the risk that he'll one day take that phone number offered to him by an attractive woman.

When you fail to meet your lifemate's needs, when your lifemate fails to meet yours, or when you both fail at this mission, the person left wanting more looks to have those needs taken care of in some other way. Unfortunately, this can lead to infidelity in many marriages. For other couples, it leads to one or both of them diverting the time, energy, and emotion that should be invested in their marriage into other activities or relationships. For others still, it leads to discontent, constant arguing, or indifference. None of that makes for a lasting, happy marriage.

Your marriage cannot be your last priority. It takes work to make sure your lifemate's needs are met—particularly as military members. Those of you who wear the uniform put a lot of passion and effort into your jobs. You strive to be the best at what you do. You go to training, trying to become the best warriors you can be. As you master combat skills, you can get so caught up making a living that you forget you're making a life together with your lifemate. All too frequently, couples get so caught up in the job, school, and that second job—not to mention the kids—that their marriage falls down into last place. You can find yourself giving your all and the best of you at work, while giving your lifemate and your family your leftovers. They deserve more than that.

For a long time, I (Michael) gave my family my leftovers, meeting my wife's needs only as much as it was convenient for me. I was in a demanding job and focused on building a successful career, and I made that my priority. Even though she deserved the best of me, Myra wasn't getting it. I eventually figured out I was risking my marriage and made significant changes to make sure her needs were met. What drove this drastic transformation within me? The catalyst came, as Matthew 21:16 says, "out of the mouths of babes." One Sunday, I was engaged in the mindless repetitive activity of channel surfing. When our daughter Lindsay, who was only six years old, asked me a question, I responded with a noncommittal "Uh-huh" because I wasn't giving her my undivided attention.

Lindsay was and is a lot like me, her father. She possessed excellent people skills even at the early age of six. She knew I wasn't really listening to her, so she slowly positioned herself between me and the television and looked directly in my eyes. Once she had my attention, Lindsay said, "Daddy, you're not listening to me." That's what did it. That was a stake-in-the-ground moment that made me realize I needed to change my ways and be a more present father for my girls and a more present husband for my wife. From that day on, I was more intentional about displacing any negative memories of the "leftover" dad and husband with new, positive memories.

Naturally, there'll be times when you need to put your own needs on hold and be patient with your spouse and times when your spouse does the same for you. If one of you is deployed, you simply can't be there to meet all those needs for each other in the moment. If one of you is ill or called away to care for an ailing parent, you can't be fully present for your lifemate. Fortunately, those times should be the exception over the course of your relationship, and they should always be temporary. A short period of time in which you can't be there for each other shouldn't harm your marriage. Do the best you can while you're apart, and when you come back together, get back to being the one person in the world your lifemate knows will selflessly put their needs first.

Create Your LifeM8Z Moment

1. Ask your mate to write a list of ten ways for you to meet his or her needs, while you do the same. When you're done, exchange lists and take turns discussing each item to ensure you fully understand the details of what your mate means.

2. Sit hand-in-hand, eye-to-eye, and knee-to-knee with your lifemate and discuss how you would each like the other to inform you when one or more of your needs isn't being met.

3. With your mate, make a list of ten things each of you can do to ensure your marriage remains a passionate priority.

CHAPTER 3

Adopt a Winning Mindset

Until you've lived it, you have no idea what to expect. Military life is like no other lifestyle. In order to be successful, active-duty service members must immerse themselves in their profession. This commitment to arms is captured in the "Soldier's Creed" of the Army, Navy, Air Force, and Marine Corps. It clearly illustrates the mindset needed to thrive in the military. However, that mindset can be hard for other people, including the family of service members, to accept and comprehend. Military spouses can gain a better understanding of the mental and physical demands and responsibilities of those who proudly wear the uniform and have sworn their allegiance by taking time to study the "Soldier's Creed."

I am an American Soldier.

I am a warrior and a member of a team.

I serve the people of the United States, and live the Army Values.

I will always place the mission first.

I will never accept defeat.

I will never quit.

I will never leave a fallen comrade.

I am disciplined, physically and mentally tough, trained and proficient in my warrior tasks and drills.

I always maintain my arms, my equipment and myself.

I am an expert and I am a professional.

I stand ready to deploy, engage, and destroy, the enemies of the United States of America in close combat.

I am a guardian of freedom and the American way of life.

I am an American Soldier.

(Source: www.army.mil/values/soldiers.html)

There can be no doubt that this ethos is part of what makes this country great. It clearly defines the mindset you must bring to your work as a member of the armed services. But one question bears asking: *How does this "Soldier's Creed" impact the military dependent family?* While the commitment to their service and the expectations of the military member are clear, there's no mention of the balance required to serve your nation and your family at the same time. We created the "Warrior-Spouse Ethos" to establish a set of expectations that complement the "Soldier's Creed," providing a service-home-life balance for military families.

Let it serve as a reminder of your most important commitments.

We are a Military Family.

We work as a Warrior-Team to support our military member and maintain the family.

We serve the people of the United States and our family.

We will always place the mission first while striving to ensure the needs of our military member and our family are met.

We will never accept defeat.

We will never quit.

We will never give up on our family.

We are disciplined, physically and mentally tough, and trained and proficient to overcome any challenge that may face us when separated by deployment or when united at the home front.

We will work hard to maintain the right balance between our military commitments, our relationship, and our family.

We will always guard our hearts and our fidelity to each other.

We stand ready to face deployments and new duty assignments, and we will engage, neutralize, and repel any and all threats to our family.

We are guardians of freedom and the American way of life.

We are devoted spouses, and we are devoted to our family.

We undertook this journey together, and we will finish it together.

We are a Military Family, and we work as a Warrior-Team to support our military member and maintain the family.

WHY MINDSET MATTERS

When Porsha married Daryl, she knew he wouldn't be making a lot of money since he was just at the beginning of his military career. However, Porsha had grown up in a fairly wealthy family, and she was accustomed to getting the material things she desired. Not long after they married, she started to feel dissatisfied because Daryl couldn't provide her with a lavish lifestyle. Once the reality that her husband really couldn't give her what she wanted sank in, Porsha was disappointed. She complained to her family that Daryl wasn't meeting her expectations. Accustomed to providing for her, Porsha's father offered to step in and buy his baby girl whatever she was missing. Porsha accepted the offer.

Imagine the problem that decision created in Porsha and Daryl's household. Daryl wanted to be the provider for his family, and he was. He made sure they had all the must-haves, but unfortunately for his wife, he wasn't able to provide some of the nice-to-haves she insisted on. When he found out she'd gone to her father, Daryl felt like his wife was trying to emasculate him. The marriage became strained, and Daryl eventually had an affair. As so often happens, Porsha found out about her husband's infidelity, and there was major fallout in their marriage. In the end, Porsha and Daryl were able to save their marriage, but the quality of their relationship suffered.

They both went through a lot of heartache that could've been easily avoided. No marriage is without its trials, but their major problem could've been nipped in the bud if either one of them had brought a winning mindset to their marriage. What if Porsha had seen herself as becoming selfless in her marriage instead of focusing on what Daryl could buy her? And what if he had been proactive and talked about marriage expectations with the goal of preemptively repelling threats like infidelity before they could occur in the marriage? If either one of them had adopted a winning mindset for their marriage, the infidelity could've been avoided, and they could've both sidestepped a lot of unnecessary struggle and pain.

Your marriage mindset consists of your thoughts, beliefs, and attitudes about yourself, your lifemate, and the institution of marriage. That mindset determines what you believe is possible for your marriage, and that belief determines how you behave in your marriage and the results you get. Adopting a winning mindset is an essential skill in fighting for your military marriage.

Over the years, we've discovered ten mindsets that work together to form a winning mindset for your marriage. They are:

1. I can master the art of love.
2. I choose open communication with my lifemate.
3. I'm committed to growing and changing for the better.
4. I'm becoming selfless in my marriage.
5. We overcome challenges together.
6. I repel all threats to our marriage.
7. I always choose forgiveness.
8. I value true intimacy in my marriage.
9. My lifemate is my best friend.
10. I'm proud to share our success with other couples.

THE FIRST MINDSET: I CAN MASTER THE ART OF LOVE

Every Sunday, the same scenario played out at our house. I (Michael) would be ready for church, sitting in the car, determined to be on time. While Myra was inside, getting herself and our young daughter dressed for church, I was in the driveway, honking the horn and growing more impatient by the minute. Week after week, we went through the same thing, and it never occurred to me that things might move along a little faster if I went inside and helped my wife. I wasn't practicing the art of love in my marriage (because I didn't know what it was at that time), and it caused a lot of unnecessary friction and frustration.

Many couples struggle to define love in their marriage, but you can find the perfect definition of love in 1 Corinthians 13:4-8a (NIV), which reads, "Love is patient, love is kind. It does not envy, it does not boast, it is not proud. It does not dishonor others, it is not self-seeking, it is not easily angered, it keeps no record of wrongs. Love does not delight in evil but rejoices with the truth. It always protects, always trusts, always hopes, always perseveres. Love never fails."

If you want to master the art of love, make this a self-assessment by replacing the word "love" with the word "I" in that passage.

I am patient.

I am kind.

I do not envy.

I do not boast.

I am not proud.

I do not dishonor others.

I am not self-seeking.

I am not easily angered.

I keep no record of wrongs.

I do not delight in evil but rejoice with the truth.

I always protect.

I always trust.

I always hope.

I always persevere.

I never fail.

Love is often described as a feeling, but it's much more than that. It's a conscious decision to love through the good and the bad, regardless of the circumstances. Love is an unconditional, lifelong commitment. Love is an art form because the two of you, either purposefully or unintentionally, paint the portrait that will be your life together. The words you direct at your lifemate, the thoughts you have about her, how you treat him behind closed doors, and how you talk about each other when you're not together—these are the colors you use to paint the portrait of your marriage. You get to choose whether you'll throw together a sloppy picture you'd rather hang in the garage so no one can see it or meticulously paint a masterpiece you can't wait to put on display.

THE SECOND MINDSET: I CHOOSE OPEN COMMUNICATION WITH MY LIFEMATE

Before Omar and Pam got married, they talked about the demands of military life. She was an educator and could find work almost anywhere, so they agreed his career would take priority in their family. When Omar got an opportunity to move from a desk job to an operational unit, Pam encouraged him and reiterated that she would support him in building his career. Unfortunately, Pam didn't fully realize everything that came along with the new job. Omar had to be prepared to do a lot of training and a lot of traveling, sometimes at short notice. As the years wore on, Pam began to feel resentful. She felt like her husband was constantly leaving her to deal with the kids on her own. The reality of the situation, which she continued to claim to support, wasn't at all what she'd expected.

Finally, Omar probed his wife a bit about her change in attitude. Pam was able to honestly confess to him that she'd been struggling with the amount of family responsibility that fell on her. With open dialogue, they were able to get back to their agreed-upon priorities. Pam recognized that this was what she had signed up for and there was nothing useful about being bitter. Omar agreed to continue to include her in major decisions. The couple was able to stop the downward slide of their marriage simply by sharing their thoughts and feelings and seeking to understand and support each other.

Notice that Omar and Pam didn't just talk. Talking isn't necessarily communicating. Effective communication requires you and your lifemate to connect, understand, and be understood. Learning to communicate is crucial to a successful marriage because, over the years, you'll both change (and hopefully grow). When you say, "I do," you marry three people: 1) the person your lifemate was before you met, 2) the person your lifemate is when you marry, and 3) the person your lifemate will become as the result of you being in his or her life. If you fail to communicate over the course of your relationship, you'll find yourself married to a stranger.

If you've ever seen a couple go through a twenty-year divorce, you know what we mean. The couple spends two decades putting all their energy into raising their kids and building their careers. Once the kids are gone, the husband and wife find they have little in common. They barely even know each other anymore. In fact, they may not even like each other very much. If they're not willing to do the work to come back together, they're doomed to suffer through a mediocre marriage for the rest of their lives, or they'll eventually call it quits.

We see it happen all the time, but it doesn't have to be that way. Because we made our marriage a priority even while we were raising our kids, we're happy empty nesters. Because we worked on our communication skills and used them to maintain our connection, we counted down to the moment when the kids were grown and gone. We love being parents, but we celebrated when the last one moved out! For us, it was an opportunity to spend more time together and focus on each other (and leave the bedroom door open and make as much noise as we want).

You communicate with words, but you also communicate non-verbally through touch, eye contact, and tone of voice. Awareness of all of these factors can greatly improve the communication in your marriage. That's where one of our favorite techniques, the simple but powerful hand-in-hand, eye-to-eye, knee-to-knee communication technique, comes in. When you use it consistently and with an open mind, it can be a game changer for your marriage.

As a teenager, I (Michael) studied various forms of martial arts, including taekwondo, hapkido, and sei kendo kai. They all share a basic stance, which provides the fighter a stable position to harness the power, speed, and mobility needed to respond effectively to any situation that might confront him. We encourage you to make the hand-in-hand, eye-to-eye, and knee-to-knee communication technique your basic communication stance. Use this technique as your safe environment to talk about what's going well in the relationship, what needs to be improved, and what needs to be added or eliminated to allow the relationship to grow and blossom. Find a situation or two in your relationship to discuss and practice this new tool so you can be ready to use it when you really need it.

This is a powerful technique that we use with every couple we see. When couples talk about their issues or challenges, we have them explore what's going on while sitting hand-in-hand, eye-to-eye, and knee-to-knee. In that posture, you create an atmosphere for tempers to stay in control. You're more likely to talk to each other in a loving fashion that helps you to produce a win-win-win solution: a win for the husband, a win for the wife, and a win for their relationship and their family.

THE THIRD MINDSET: I'M COMMITTED TO GROWING AND CHANGING FOR THE BETTER

When Carla told us she'd made the decision to move out of her family home, we were saddened but not surprised. She had tried to get him to work on their marriage with her, but her husband, Fred, had made it clear that he didn't see the need to do anything differently. Even though he had certainly changed in many ways since they'd said, "I do," he didn't see any reason why he should *intentionally* change. When Carla finally gave up and moved out, Fred was all broken up about it, but his wife had given him the opportunity to fix things, and he'd chosen not to. His mindset kept him stuck in his ways, and it cost him his marriage.

Whether you're prepared for it or not, change is going to happen. You will change. Your lifemate will change. The world around you will change, and your marriage will change. Growth, on the other hand, is being intentional about how you want to change and what you want to achieve. If you don't commit to growth with your lifemate, you risk losing him or her. It will require you to get out of your comfort zone, but if you remember the mission of your marriage—to make sure your lifemate's needs are met—you'll see that intentional growth is essential to completing the mission.

People want to be happy, and most people will eventually get tired of being with someone who isn't willing to help them get that happiness. You can't just go along to get along in your marriage, especially when your lifemate is specifically asking you to make a change. This is a need crying out to be met, and ignoring it is a big mistake. We've found that the worst thing you can do is sign up for a session of marriage coaching, come to the session, and then do nothing to grow. That sends the message to your lifemate that you don't care. You're saying, I love you, *but*. I love you, *but not enough to do the work*. I love you, *but not enough to look honestly at myself*. I love you, *but not enough to change who I am and how I behave for you*.

THE FOURTH MINDSET: I'M BECOMING SELFLESS IN MY MARRIAGE

John and Linda had been married for more than a decade when they came to us with a problem. After tapping the family's resources to buy a new dining room set, John felt like it was his turn. He wanted to invest a few thousand dollars to create a man cave in the basement, a place he could have just for himself. John thought it was only fair since they'd just purchased a new dining room set for Linda, but she saw it differently. The dining room set was for the whole family, not just for her. Besides, she wanted to spend more time with John, not less, and she predicted that the man cave would mean less time together for the two of them. Our goal was to get them to go from "I, me, and my," to "we, us, and our." We wanted them to embrace an attitude of selflessness in their marriage.

We're all born selfish. Infants want to be fed, they want to be changed, they want to be held, they want to be rocked, they want everything, and they want it now! Unchecked, that same selfish nature stays with you throughout your life. As you mature into a single adult, you possess an "I, me, and my" mindset. But if you want to have a successful marriage, you have to shift to a "we, us, and our" focus. This is a major step forward in the process of the two of you becoming one.

It's perfectly fine to have a man cave or a she shed or something special that's just for you and not normally shared with your lifemate. If it works for both of you, then it's okay to have a girls' or guys' night out with your friends or to go on trips with your same-sex buddies. It only becomes a problem when that special solo activity or possession starts to drive a wedge between the two of you. When you let your desires become more important than making sure your lifemate's needs are met, you revert to the selfishness of an infant.

The easiest way to become selfless in your marriage is to focus on serving your lifemate. Make it your private, personal goal to overserve your spouse. Don't keep a record of what you do for each other, but strive to win at the game of serving and then have fun with that competition even if your lifemate knows nothing about it. Thirty-nine years into our marriage, we still strive to wow each other whenever we can, and that effort helps us to each stay focused on meeting the other's needs. In the end, we both win, and the marriage wins.

We can't ignore the reality that, in many households, the wives do a lot for their husbands by virtue of the way household responsibilities are divided. Wives, selflessness means going a step farther and finding ways, big and small, to cater to your husband. At the same time, a selfless husband will do the same for you. Ephesians 5:22 tells wives to submit themselves to their husbands. Most people stop right there when they discuss biblical marriage, and it starts a big fight. However, if you continue to read, that chapter goes on to instruct husbands to love your wives as Christ loved the Church. He so loved the Church that He was willing to die for it, and that willingness to sacrifice is what selflessness looks like. Husbands, be willing to lay down your life, your ego, and your selfish ways for your wife.

THE FIFTH MINDSET: WE OVERCOME CHALLENGES TOGETHER

Mark and Tia were living in a marriage rocked by multiple infidelities. As we talked with them, we discovered that Mark, who had committed the adultery, had suffered serious abuse during his childhood. His struggle required deeper help than we could give, and we referred him to a qualified professional. Mark and Tia continued to see us for marriage coaching for a while, and then they dropped off. Two years later, we crossed paths with Tia, who updated us on their situation.

Mark had continued in therapy to deal with and heal from the abuse he'd experienced. He'd stopped cheating, and Tia had chosen to love him through that whole process. They were happier than ever. They went through the fire together, and their marriage came out stronger because of the work they put into healing, repenting, and forgiving. The infidelity didn't make their marriage better, but their response to it did.

Every marriage will come up against obstacles. Some will be behavioral, some relational, financial, or health related. The key is to not let these challenges tear you two apart. Instead, use conflict to bring you closer together and strengthen the bonds of your relationship. Remember that you can't fix everything, but you can fix anything you focus on. When an obstacle arises, give it the attention and effort required to get past it. Focus on it and deal with it—not alone, but as a team—until it becomes the strongest link in your relationship. Repeat the process for every new challenge you face. Do this again and again, and your relationship will gradually grow stronger and stronger over time.

THE SIXTH MINDSET: I REPEL ALL THREATS TO OUR MARRIAGE

I (Michael) had traveled to DC alone for work, and I was eating in the hotel restaurant when a woman approached me. She smiled and slid into a chair to join me at my table. "Are you staying here?" she asked.

"Actually," I told her, "I'm married."

Her smile grew bigger. "I don't care," she said.

I did care, and I excused myself. For the rest of that trip, I bought a sandwich for dinner and ate it in my room. Years earlier, I might have sat and enjoyed a meal with the woman, flirting with her a little and allowing her to flirt with me, but by then, I understood the danger that presented. I knew that kind of behavior was hurtful to my wife and could open the door to something more. Even if she'd never know about it, I didn't want to do anything that would hurt Myra. I had prepared myself so that when the threat came at my marriage, I recognized it and handled it easily.

In peacetime, we prepare for war. Military organizations and first responders conduct exercises during times of calm. They run drills in mock-up buildings; they practice combat maneuvers. They train, again and again, under realistic conditions to ensure they operate smoothly and efficiently as an integrated team. Success is only achieved when each team member is highly proficient in their role and can automatically perform as an integral part of the team.

If you wait until your marriage is under attack to do something about possible threats, you're going to have a much tougher fight on your hands, and it's one you might lose. You must prepare in advance by understanding what your vulnerabilities are. You have to acknowledge the weaknesses in your relationship and your own individual weaknesses. Early in our marriage, my (Michael's) weaknesses were alcohol, flirta-tiousness, poorly defined boundaries, and not having a good understanding of what I'd signed up for when I said, "I do." As I began to recognize those weaknesses, I had a choice. I could choose to do something about them, or I could continue to put my marriage at risk.

This mindset—I repel all threats to our marriage—goes back to looking at the man (or woman) in the mirror. You have to be absolutely honest with yourself. If you have an issue with pornography, alcohol or drugs, compulsive spending, gambling, a secret social media life, or any other behavior that could be a threat to your marriage, you need to acknowledge it and commit to permanent change before it causes permanent damage. Even if you're not actively engaged in the destructive behavior at the moment, you have to be proactive and address it because, left unchecked, it can show up when you least expect it.

Take infidelity for example. Typically, the decision to cheat is a slow slide from faithfulness to adultery. It starts with shared looks across the parking lot when you arrive at work in the mornings. But then you see her inside, and she's always at the coffee bar. Now, you make it a point to be at the coffee bar at that same time every day—and you take just a little more time getting ready for work each morning. One day, you say hello, and the two of you share a table while you have your latte and a blueberry muffin. That ten minutes together becomes a part of your morning routine, and you start to look forward to it. You arrange to have lunch alone with her a few days a week, and then you find out you'll both be attending the same conference. At the conference, you're staying in the same hotel, on the same floor, and you ask her if she wants to have dinner with you, in your hotel room, after a long day. There she sits, at the foot of your bed, just waiting for you. You've reached a decision point. What will you do?

In that scenario, you've put yourself in a difficult position. You have to choose, in that moment of temptation, to be unfaithful or to tell this woman, who you've been giving your attention to for days or weeks, to get out of your room. It never had to get to that point because you could've stopped it anywhere along the way. If you know flirtation is an issue for you, and you acknowledge it as a character flaw, you can do the work to change it long before it becomes a problem. When that woman smiles at you in the parking lot, you can give her a professional "good morning" nod and go about your business without giving her another thought. (We're using a man as an example here, but it could just as easily be a wife sliding into infidelity the same way.)

It's easy to say, "Well, I can't help who flirts with me," or "It just sort of happened," but that takes all the ownership and control away from you and your lifemate. When you change your thinking and embrace this mindset—I repel all threats to our marriage—you acknowledge that no external threat can harm your relationship unless you let it. You are in control.

THE SEVENTH MINDSET: I ALWAYS CHOOSE FORGIVENESS

Every success story we share in *Fighting for Your Military Marriage* required forgiveness on some level. Whenever one of you becomes complacent in your marriage, you fall short of your marriage mission, and that always requires forgiveness. You have to be willing to forgive yourself when you fall short, and you have to be willing to forgive your lifemate when he or she does too.

Anyone who's been wronged or hurt understands how hard the thought of forgiving can be. It can be tempting, but dangerous, to cling to unforgiveness as a means of self-protection or to punish the offender. Three things define unforgiveness, and two of them can be destructive to your marriage:

1. Retaliation: You will pay for this.
2. Resentment: I am angry and I don't like you very much right now.
3. Resurgence: I will never forget.

To forgive means to release feelings of anger and the desire for revenge. It doesn't mean you have to forget what happened. In fact, remembering can be useful when it's done for the right reasons.

Someone has done you wrong, and every time she enters the room, your blood begins to boil and your head feels like it will explode. In that situation, the anger, frustration, and resentment you feel only hurts you. The individual who triggered that response in you probably doesn't have a clue what you're feeling. In fact, you may be holding on to something your offender has forgotten or totally moved on from. At its heart, forgiveness isn't as much for the offender as it is for the offended party, the one who believes they have been wronged. As spiritual leader Marianne Williamson says, "Unforgiveness is like drinking poison and waiting for the other person to die."

When you sit in negative emotion and hostility directed at your lifemate, you cause yourself and your marriage unnecessary stress. On the other hand, when you choose to forgive your lifemate, the act of forgiveness frees you and your marriage from the baggage associated with revenge and resentment. Remembering can be used for good or evil. Remembering a transgression from a place of unforgiveness can turn it into a blunt instrument you use to beat up your spouse. However, remembering so you can do everything in your power to make sure that particular problem doesn't have another chance to attack your relationship can be like a personal defense weapon for your marriage.

In our work and in our own marriage, we've witnessed the power of forgiveness. But people often ask us, "Aren't some acts unforgivable?" Our answer: "Maybe." But most of the things you think of as unforgivable actually don't have to be. Deal-breakers make good talk-show fodder, but in truth, you have no idea whether or not a situation will be a deal-breaker for you until you're faced with it.

Don't misunderstand us. If you're being abused, you have to protect yourself. Get out of the situation and find a safe place for you and your children. If your spouse is having sex with multiple partners and putting you at risk for sexually transmitted diseases, some of which still have no cure, you may have to leave to keep yourself out of harm's way. Those are extreme situations, and they may call for extreme action, but the most common transgression people describe as a deal-breaker is adultery. Many people believe infidelity will be an obvious deal-breaker for them—until they find themselves at that crossroads. Your spouse has admitted to an affair or you've found out about it. Do you throw it all away? Or do you fight for your marriage? Faced with that decision, things seldom seem so black and white.

For many couples, faith is at the root of their ability to forgive each other. They look to Jesus as the example. When He was asked, "How many times shall I forgive?" He answered, "Until seventy times seven" (Matthew 18:22, KJV). We take that to mean there's no limit on the number of times you forgive a transgression. You take this burden you've been carrying, and you lay it at the foot of the cross and walk away. This includes forgiving yourself or someone else just as God has forgiven you.

Yes, you should forgive, but should you forget? No. We want you to remember, not to keep digging up old hurts, but to allow yourself to look back and see how far you've come.

THE EIGHTH MINDSET: I VALUE TRUE INTIMACY IN MY MARRIAGE

It's important to your marriage that you embrace a desire for true intimacy in your relationship with your lifemate. When we hear on TV or in the movies that two people "were intimate," it usually refers to sex, but true intimacy is so much more. True intimacy is only achieved when you're able to step into each other's worlds and see the real person inside your spouse. To do this, you must listen, endeavor to understand, and accept and affirm your lifemate's viewpoint without judgment.

Create **social intimacy** with your lifemate by sharing a common set of friends. The people you hang out with most of the time should be other married couples. Hanging out with single people, who are still pursuing the opposite sex, can cause a problem for married people, so that shouldn't be your main social interaction. When you socialize as a couple, you build on your friendship, and you develop shared interests that bring you and your lifemate even closer.

Intellectual intimacy develops in your relationship when you're willing to share your thoughts, opinions, and perceptions with each other without judgment. When you accept and respect your differences, you develop a deeper layer of trust. You can discuss anything from politics to parenting, career goals, books, movies, or the meaning of life itself. As long as you're willing to give each other your undivided attention and unbiased understanding, these discussions will deepen your shared intimacy on an intellectual level.

When you and your spouse regularly share your personal feelings and deep emotions, you create a sacred space in which you can share things you might never tell anyone else. That **emotional intimacy** strengthens the bond of trust in your relationship. The more you honor each other by showing compassion and acceptance for each other's feelings, the more emotional intimacy you'll share.

Financial intimacy requires complete transparency when it comes to your money. Sharing your strengths and weaknesses in money management allows you and your lifemate to work together to help each other grow in this area. You can develop joint financial strategies, including spending thresholds and guidelines for getting each other's consent to spend larger amounts of money. Together, you can create and achieve financial goals that serve your family. Money is a hot-button issue for many couples, so getting on the same page and creating financial intimacy will strengthen your marriage.

Physical intimacy refers to the kind of non-sexual touch you use to express your closeness to and affection for each other. Your skin is your largest organ, and human beings are designed to respond to loving touch. Sit close together on the couch and put your arms around each other. Hold each other close and dance in the kitchen. Cuddle and spoon in bed. Physical intimacy also includes being open with your lifemate about your physical health and wellbeing and sharing any challenges or struggles you face in this area. Don't try to deal with a diagnosis or medical concern alone. Those obstacles should be overcome together.

God's plan for marriage is for you and your lifemate to grow together spiritually, minister to each other, minister to other couples, and build a marriage that glorifies Him. When you follow that plan, you develop **spiritual intimacy** in your marriage. You and your spouse can connect on a spiritual level in a unique way. And for many couples, bringing together your individual relationships with God to form a relationship between God and your marriage is essential to building a lasting and satisfying marriage.

Finally, we come to **sexual intimacy**. This level of intimacy is unique because it's reserved to be shared exclusively with your lifemate. You may have some level of social or emotional intimacy, for example, with your friends, but sexual intimacy is just for your marriage. The biological purpose of sexual intimacy is procreation, but it can provide so much more. It's key to creating a marriage rich in companionship, pleasure, and commitment to each other.

A marriage without true intimacy is a shallow existence haunted by unfulfilled potential. It might look good on the outside. You can have a nice car, a nice house, and a beautiful little Jack Russell terrier, but a marriage without intimacy lacks passion and commitment. When you have true intimacy in your relationship, you create the oneness you were designed to have with your spouse. You get to live your relationship out loud without fear of rejection or judgment from the person you've chosen to spend the rest of your life loving.

THE NINTH MINDSET: MY LIFEMATE IS MY BEST FRIEND

I (Michael) find it difficult to say no, which occasionally causes me to overcommit. I love to give back, but each endeavor comes with regular commitments. These commitments and the associated preparation take time, and time is a precious commodity. As much as I like making a difference in my community, I'd rather be home with my lifemate, Myra. There's no one else I'd rather hang out with. We're best friends, and we enjoy spending time together even when we just stay in the house, put on our comfy clothes, and watch our favorite horror films. There's just nowhere else I'd rather be. (If that makes me whipped, then I'm whipped and proud of it!)

When you look at what a best friend is, it makes sense that your lifemate should fulfill that role in your life. Your best friend wants the best for you. He or she is always striving to help you grow and evolve. Your best friend is your biggest cheerleader, always encouraging you to spread your wings and fly in the direction of your goals. When the two of you disagree, you can do it passionately and still maintain your friendship. Your best friend is the person you most want to spend time with and the person you can tell all your secrets to, and you have more fun hanging out with your best friend than you do with anyone else. When you have good news or when you need help with a problem, your best friend is the person you can't wait to talk to. Your best friend sees a side of you that few people get to see.

If your lifemate isn't your best friend, someone else will be. When you're best friends with someone other than your spouse, you take a part of yourself away from your spouse and give it to that person. You divide your intimacy, your time, your trust, and your attention between your lifemate and that best friend. If your best friend is a member of the opposite sex, it can cause problems in your marriage even when there's no infidelity going on. Your lifemate may struggle to trust that your relationship is platonic, or he or she may just resent the fact that you're willing to be that close with someone outside of your marriage.

Of course, you'll have close friends besides your lifemate, but choosing to make your lifemate your best friend adds an element of trust and an element of fun to your marriage. If you and your lifemate haven't been best friends thus far, you can change that. Husbands, start to think of your wife as your best friend. Wives, think of your husband in the same way. Tell other people that your lifemate is your best friend forever and start to act that way.

THE TENTH MINDSET: I'M PROUD TO SHARE OUR SUCCESS WITH OTHER COUPLES

Once I (Michael) finished my technical training at Vandenberg, we moved to Montana. On my first day, I walked into the squadron, and the very first person I met was a six-foot-three, big, intimidating guy who I'd later learn had played college football. He stood up and looked at me, and then a warm, friendly smile spread across his face as he chuckled. "Boy," he said, "I'm gonna take care of you." That moment was the start of a lifelong friendship.

Dan White and his wife, Gwen, really took us under their wing. They invited us to church with them, and they became our friends and our role models. We had a standing invitation to the White House, as we liked to call it, for Thanksgiving and Christmas. We were there with them when they had their first son. They also adopted two girls, and the choice to grow their family in that way made an impression on us. We started looking at adoption and were going through the process when I was transferred to Langley. That experience prepared us. And when the situation presented itself, we were ready to welcome Myra's niece, Ashlei, into our home.

The White's provided us with a living model of a successful marriage. Sharing your marriage success with other couples is like sharing the good news. A lot of couples have lost hope and are just limping along until they can figure out how to end their marriage. They don't think they can ever love each other again. Others still love each other, but they're missing the tools, techniques, or faith to make it through. They're ready to bail at the first sign of turbulence when all they really need is some guidance or an example of a couple doing the work. These couples need you to share what you've overcome and how you manage to remain happily married just as Dan and Gwen shared with us.

Popular culture doesn't provide many examples of successful marriages. In the movies, the credits roll as the romantic-comedy couple finally gets together and wedding bells ring. You don't see what happens after they say, "I do." In dramas, husbands and wives scheme behind each other's backs or barely put up with each other. The couples having the hot, steamy love-making scenes aren't married—unless they're married to other people and having an affair. Your marriage can be the antidote to all of the potentially poisonous messages about marriage presented by the media.

You don't need to have a perfect marriage to share your success with other couples. We love it when people tell us, "We want what you've got." We take it as a compliment. But as much as we enjoy it when couples look to us as a model for marriage, we also know the perfect marriage doesn't exist. A good marriage takes work, and commitment, and a real investment of your time and energy. That's the message we want to share with you, and it's the message we want you to share with other couples.

Our marriage is also creating a legacy for our kids. When our firstborn daughter, Lindsay, went off to college, her friends had a hard time believing her parents had been married for twenty-five years and were still going strong, and yet, here we are. It's also a legacy for the larger community. We want every married couple to know this kind of lasting love is available to them too. Let your marriage create the same kind of legacy.

You don't have to be married twenty-five years before you start sharing your success. Dan and Gwen are only a few years older than we are, but they still served as role models for us. They're at the center of a ripple effect of positive impact on the marriages we've touched. Every couple we help owes a bit of gratitude to the Whites. Even in the most informal way, you can choose to make a difference for couples who struggle where you thrive. Once you've broken the code and unlocked most of the doors to a successful military marriage, you're ready to share your success with other couples. Everything you've experienced and the challenges you've overcome have prepared you to share your wisdom with others. Find a younger couple to mentor or find any other couple who could benefit from having positive role models like you in their lives.

Every time we conduct a seminar or sit down to coach a couple, it's a marriage enrichment moment for us. We get to tell our story again, and when we tell it, we feel all the emotion that goes with it. You'll discover that sharing your success with other couples will help you appreciate what you have together even more. It will strengthen your grasp of the tools and ideas you've used to make it this far. Ultimately, you'll benefit as much as, or even more than, the couples you mentor.

It doesn't matter if you have a rock-solid relationship or a relationship that's somehow gotten off-track. If you sincerely practice taking on these mindsets, you'll see dramatic improvements in your marriage. You'll get to the place where you know that you know *that you know* your marriage will make it. For most people, these are new ways of thinking about marriage, and they may take a while to get used to. Practice believing them and applying them, and they'll become second nature. Remember that each mindset is a key to unlock the series of doors leading to a life of connection, love, trust, and intimacy.

Create Your LifeM8Z Moment

1. Review the "Warrior-Spouse Ethos" and share with your mate what each attribute means to you.

2. How well have you mastered the art of love? Ask your mate to identify the top three needs they would like you to work on, and you do the same for them. Make those three needs your prayer targets for the next month. In thirty days, meet again to discuss how you've changed and grown in the art of love.

3. Commit to sitting down every day, hand-in-hand, eye-to-eye, and knee-to-knee, to connect in the following ways:

   - Reaffirm your love and commitment to each other.

   - Share the best thing that happened during your day.

   - Share something that happened during your day that was stressful or disturbing.

   - Ask, "Was there anything I did to disappoint you?"

   - Ask, "Was there anything I did to surprise or please you?"

- Reaffirm your love and commitment to each other and share how you would like to see your relationship change and grow.

4. What threats present a clear and present danger to your marriage? What actions do you need to take, what do you need to change, and what commitments do you need to make to neutralize those threats and preserve your marriage?

5. Review the seven types of intimacy and agree upon specific actions you, as a couple, can take to strengthen each one.

CHAPTER 4

Be a Person of Integrity

I (Michael) was a Class B Bachelor for about six months. I reported to Colorado Springs for my job as a test director in January and moved into a downtown apartment while Myra and the kids were back in Virginia finishing out the school year. I arranged some flights home over those months, but for the most part, I was on my own. Knowing my outgoing nature and knowing that an idle mind is the devil's playground, I made it a point to keep myself busy. In the early weeks, I stayed at work late every day. But then I realized my team felt obligated to stay as late as I did. Rather than let that be an excuse to get out of my office earlier, I asked my secretary to knock on my door at five o'clock every evening and remind me it was time to go. After work, I'd go work out and then come back to the office after everyone else had left for the day. I filled my free time with productive activity. I went to church, and I joined the men's ministry and the men's chorus. I was very intentional about not having idle time.

One Saturday, I went to work out and then spent a few hours working in my office. When I got back home, there was an attractive young woman sitting on the steps of my apartment complex. In an instant, the thought went through my mind, "Michael, just say hello and keep walking." Because I'm a friendly, extroverted guy, it's my nature to want to strike up a conversation in a situation like that. That's fine when you're single, but as a married man, I knew it could create a problem. At the very least, I could have given that woman the wrong impression about my interest in her.

When Myra and I spoke on the phone, I told her about that moment. The devil knows you and the devil knows exactly what your weakness is. That was a test I passed, and knowing I had the fortitude to do the right thing when it counted made me proud of myself. Those moments of self-discipline can help you clearly see your potential to be your best you. Even better, the next time something comes up, that moment of success makes it easier for you to do the right thing. Becoming self-disciplined in my marriage and honoring my vows no matter what gave me a deep sense of satisfaction. When I moved from being the flirtatious guy to becoming a man Myra could trust, I could honestly say I was proud of the kind of husband I was.

When I (Myra) saw Michael choosing to focus only on me when we were out together, I began to believe he was really becoming more self-disciplined. It gave me the sense that he was truly changed, and I began to trust that he would also be self-disciplined when we were apart. It would be impossible for me to be with him all the time, and the change in his behavior encouraged me to believe I could trust him at work or at functions. I no longer had to worry about him flirting with other women or doing anything that would put our marriage at risk. He was a man of integrity.

Proverbs 10:9 (ESV) says, "Whoever walks in integrity walks securely, but he who makes his ways crooked will be found out." A person of integrity is a man or woman of character and honor. When you decide to live your life as a person of integrity, you commit to doing what you say you're going to do. You choose to do the right thing even when nobody's around to witness your choice. In your marriage, being a person of integrity means you live up to your vows. At the heart of being a person of integrity is self-discipline. It's a character trait you can and should develop to protect your marriage.

Self-discipline is choosing to do the right thing because it is right, even when it's hard or you don't feel like doing it. It's the ability to delay gratification. Self-discipline is ingrained in every military member. An Airman doesn't like guarding an aircraft on a tarmac when it's 110 degrees and there's no relief from the rays of the sun. A Soldier isn't thrilled about today's sixteen-mile hike with a sixty-five-pound rucksack. Most Sailors don't look forward to a midnight-to-four watch shift. Let's face it—there are things in life that we'd much rather avoid, but our character, self-discipline, and moral compass allow us to resist instant gratification in favor of long-term gain. Bring that same self-discipline you've developed in the military to bear in your marriage and you will drastically increase your chances of having a long and happy marriage. Successful couples share the ability to discipline their minds, choose their behavior, and determine their results.

YOUR LOCUS OF CONTROL

Beginning college psychology students learn about a theory known as *locus of control* that explains how individuals view their life experiences. Our perceptions, after all, shape our reality. Some people go through life believing that their destiny, good or bad, is determined by things beyond their control. This life view restricts them to a life of perpetual problems, pain, and pessimism. Other people choose lives filled with promise, purpose, and positivity. The difference between these two groups: the first group believes their fate is determined by outside forces. They have an external locus of control. The second group believes their perceptions, behaviors, and choices determine the quality of their life. They have an internal locus of control. Needless to say, the difference between these two types of people is huge.

Where individuals with an external locus of control see failure, individuals with an internal locus of control recognize opportunities to learn. Where individuals with an external locus of control see conflict, individuals with an internal locus of control see growth opportunities. Where individuals with an external locus of control see disappointment, people with an internal locus of control see forgiveness and reconciliation. The results, effects, and rewards of seeing the role your mind plays in shaping the quality of your life are limitless, especially when measured over a lifetime and particularly when applied to your marriage.

Why do some people enjoy marriages that last a lifetime while others endure a series of one failed relationship after the other? Oftentimes, the latter blame these failed attempts at commitment and love on the other individual(s). They just cannot come to the realization that they have culpability in these failures. The responsibility for failure and the capacity to enjoy a life and a marriage filled with love, passion, and joy lie within your control. You can control yourself, your life, and how well your life is lived. You do this by first accepting that your destiny is your own to create. Next, you recognize that you have the power to influence the state of your marriage. And finally, you must exercise self-discipline to become a person of integrity and create the kind of marriage you want to have.

If you haven't been a self-disciplined person in your life or in your marriage, now is the time to take control and change that. Here are ten ways to begin to develop self-discipline in your marriage.

10 TIPS FOR DEVELOPING SELF-DISCIPLINE IN MARRIAGE

1. Assume responsibility for your own actions.

2. Honestly address your personal and relationship vulnerabilities.

3. Identify three things to do each day that will make you a better lifemate.

4. Get clear about your priorities and eliminate time parasites.

5. Just because you can, doesn't mean you should.

6. Make technology work for you.

7. Focus on the most important things.

8. Make the most of your time.

9. Focus on improving your gifts.

10. Do what feels right, not just what feels good.

ASSUME RESPONSIBILITY FOR YOUR OWN ACTIONS

Through one of the characters he portrayed, Geraldine Jones, the late, great comedian Flip Wilson made the phrase "The devil made me do it" famous. Geraldine sashayed through life as a flirtatious, mischievous, playful soul. She was well-known for pushing the boundaries of proper conduct and sometimes naughtily, yet playfully, stepping over the line. Have you every stepped over the line and found yourself doing something you knew was wrong? Who did you blame? Who was responsible for your predicament? If you pointed the finger at anyone other than yourself, you need to look again, deeply within your own character. Be honest and true to your spouse and family, and be honest and true to yourself.

When you blame anyone other than yourself for the choices you make, you're just lying to yourself. Pop-up ads don't make you look at pornography. Strangers who slide into your DMs on social media don't make you respond to them. That man or woman who flirts with you in the office can't make you flirt back. Your best friend can't make you open a secret bank account and start siphoning off money from your family's resources. Your co-workers can't make you lie to your lifemate about what you did when you were out of town at that conference and everyone, including you, had too much to drink. Husbands, the fellas can't make you go to the strip club. And wives, your girlfriends can't make you give that guy your phone number.

The devil may place temptation in your way, but he can't make you do anything with it; neither can anyone else. Choose to have an internal locus of control and become the master of your own fate. Take ownership of the state of your marriage and take responsibility for your own happiness. If your marriage is struggling right now, don't become a victim, blaming the military, your spouse, your in-laws, your finances, or other external factors for the state of your marriage. Acknowledge the role you played in getting your marriage to where it is at the moment. Decide what kind of marriage you want to have, regardless of what's going on around you, and then do the work to create it.

HONESTLY ADDRESS YOUR PERSONAL AND RELATIONSHIP VULNERABILITIES

Recognizing and acknowledging your flaws and shortcomings can be a huge challenge. It requires you to honestly look at yourself and thoroughly assess who you are as a person, a spouse, a professional, and a person of faith. We challenge you to candidly search your heart and your character to identify your deepest secret habits, appetites, and desires. Consider the following questions as you do this internal audit:

- Am I tempted by pornography?
- Am I overly flirtatious with members of the opposite sex?
- Do I abuse substances, such as alcohol or drugs?
- Do I live a secret life outside of my marriage?
- Do I have improper relationships?
- Do I prioritize other things, people, and activities over my marriage?
- Do I live a secret life on social media?
- Do I withhold information, relationships, and concerns from my mate?
- Do I keep conversations about my relationship sacred, or do I discuss personal things with others?
- Do I rarely (if ever) communicate how much I value, love, respect, and cherish my mate?
- Do I remove my wedding ring when I'm on temporary duty or in a club?
- Do I fantasize about past partners?
- Do I keep numbers, emails, or pictures of old flames?

If you answered yes to any of these questions, you have a potential relationship vulnerability that must be addressed. You don't write your PIN on the back of your debit card, do you? You don't tape your computer passwords to your keyboard. Of course you don't. Doing so would create a glaring security breach that would require immediate corrective action. So it is with your relationship. Vulnerabilities are better taken care of proactively rather than recovered from after the fact. Couples in successful, long-term marriages periodically conduct relationship-assessment security sweeps to search for and identify any vulnerabilities that might erupt like a landmine if left unchecked. Be prepared to do the work to address any potential weaknesses you find before they have the chance to become a problem.

IDENTIFY THREE THINGS TO DO EACH DAY THAT MAKE YOU A BETTER LIFEMATE

Every day, identify three things you will do to become a better lifemate. Three things are just enough. Any more than that, and most people will lose focus or fall into overwhelm mode and do nothing at all. Pick two easy things and one that requires a little more time and effort. For us, one of those things is to sit together in the evenings and reflect on our day. I (Michael) have made it my mission to make Myra laugh a good hearty laugh every day.

If you're not sure what to do, think back to the things you did early in your relationship, perhaps when you were still dating. Maybe you can take the time to dress the way your lifemate likes or to make that special coffee blend in the mornings. Maybe you can find one thing to compliment your lifemate on every day or one thing for which you show your sincere appreciation. You can also ask your lifemate what he or she would like you to do. What did you do in the past that he misses now? What did she stop doing once you got married?

None of these are things you have to do. They should be things you want to do and can have fun doing. This should be a discipline you enjoy practicing each day. Don't beat yourself up if an item or two slips into the next day. Your objective is to be intentional about doing the things you need to do to be a better you and a better lifemate. If you've given it your best effort, then you've succeeded. Remember also that in our definition of perfect love we learned that love does not keep score. If you're working every day to be a better lifemate but your spouse isn't, don't worry about it. Focus on the only person you can change.

GET CLEAR ABOUT YOUR PRIORITIES AND ELIMINATE TIME PARASITES

As a couple, we're very intentional about how we use our time. On Friday afternoons, we shut down work at five o'clock and, even if we're staying in, date night begins. We don't allow clients to infringe on our date night. We have that boundary in place to ensure we continue to prioritize our marriage. We encourage the couples we work with to do something similar, but they often tell us they don't have time for a date night or to do a regular couple's check-in. If you find yourself in that position, try the following exercise. For one week, keep a log of how you use your time. Write down everything you do and the time you commit to it. Include everything from the six to eight hours you sleep to the time you spend commuting, at work, watching television, scrolling through social media, making meals, playing basketball, or talking on the phone. Every single thing you do should be accounted for in your time log.

Now make a list of the top three priorities in your marriage. Write them down, and then look at your time log and add up how much of your time is being spent on those priorities. How much of your time is being spent on things that don't serve those priorities or provide any real value? Those activities that steal time from your priorities are time parasites. If you don't have three hours for date night, but you spend six hours a week watching football or checking Instagram, you need to make some changes. Your priorities should dictate where you spend the majority of your time.

Recently, I (Michael) saw a young Master Sergeant come into the barber shop and take a seat to wait his turn. Instead of watching TV or messing around with his cell phone, the Sergeant pulled out his copy of *Study Guide for Testing to Senior Master Sergeant*. His actions demonstrated his commitment to preventing time parasites from sucking away his valuable time. While many of his peers unwisely used their time to watch ESPN, he was proactively eliminating any excuses and using all of his free time to prepare himself for success. It was obvious to me that he had made his career a priority and was intentional about using his time to advance in that area.

Like that Master Sergeant, you have more time in your schedule than you think. As you eliminate the time parasites—the unproductive or less important activities sucking up your time—you'll find you have more time for your priorities. Be clear about what those priorities are in your marriage, and develop a habit of taking care of them before you allow yourself to get caught up in distractions. Until you've addressed those top three priorities, you don't have time for those other things.

JUST BECAUSE YOU CAN DOES NOT MEAN THAT YOU SHOULD

You've probably heard the saying that character is what you do when no one is watching. Military life often creates situations in which no one is watching, and what you choose to do in those moments defines your character. Part of being a person of integrity is disciplining yourself to behave the same way whether your spouse will ever know what choices you make or not, always choosing in the best interest of your marriage. Throughout your military career you will be confronted with numerous opportunities to make a right or wrong decision, and what you decide will profoundly impact your marriage.

There will be many times when you can do something that your lifemate may never find out about. You can choose to watch pornography because it's available on your phone, which your lifemate never uses. You can choose to flirt with a co-worker because he or she is open to it. You can choose to over-indulge in substances that lower your inhibitions and cloud your judgment because everyone around you is doing the same thing and your lifemate is a thousand miles away. The world is filled with limitless things you *can* do, and as an adult, you have the freedom to do what you want. But just because you can, doesn't mean you should.

Unfortunately, many of our brothers and sisters in arms and their spouses fall victim to the temptation of infidelity, just because they can, especially during times of separation. More than the average married couple, they're put into positions where it seems like it would be incredibly easy to have a fling or an affair and their lifemate would never be the wiser. Discipline yourself to look at the costs in situations where the opportunity presents itself to do something so risky. You have the freedom to choose, and you'll have to live with whichever choice you make and the consequences that follow. Your free will is a powerful gift from God, but only if you use it to do the right things.

MAKE TECHNOLOGY WORK FOR YOU, NOT AGAINST YOU

Technology has become an integral part of our lives. People often complain about technology, but the fact is the internet, computers, and cell phones aren't good or bad in and of themselves. They're simply tools, and you get to decide whether to use them for your benefit or allow them to become a detriment to your life and your marriage. Technology has the potential to serve you or to make you serve it. It can have a good, bad, or ugly impact on your life and your marriage.

The Good: Gone are the days when the only way to keep in touch from far away was to write a letter. Now, you can call, video chat, text, or send video messages. The awesome power embedded in your cellular device allows you to stay connected with your lifemate, your family, and your friends. That tiny computer makes it easier than ever to reach out to your lifemate to say, "I miss you, and I can't wait until I get home and hold you in my arms." These little devices also allow you to be more efficient and productive. In so many ways, you have the world at your fingertips.

The Bad: Cell phones, tablets, and computers make it easy to waste valuable time by checking news sites, scrolling through social media, or playing video games. Instead of connecting with the people sitting right next to you, the internet makes it easy to be distracted, constantly dividing your attention between your family and the notifications dinging on your phone. No email, text, or phone call is more important than your loved ones or your marriage.

The Ugly: Carried to the extreme, technology can lure you into a fantasy world of games, role-playing, virtual relationships, and inappropriate relationships that make the jump to the real world when online flirtations become in-person meetings and more. Even a seemingly harmless need to constantly check in with your social media connections or games can cause you to lose the connectedness you should have with your family. The anonymity of the internet gives you the opportunity to be anyone you want to be, interact with anyone, and do whatever you desire while creating the illusion that it has nothing to do with your real life. The internet opens the door to temptation with unlimited access to pornography, hook-up apps and sites, and social media sites where you can easily create secret profiles and conduct a secret life.

Here are a few guidelines to help you keep your technology from becoming a distraction in your household:

- Don't spend more time interacting with your tech device than you do with your lifemate, family, or friends.

- Periodically set aside your cell phone for a day and devote an uninterrupted day to your spouse.

- Kiss and embrace your lifemate before you reach for your cell to check your email, text messages, Facebook posts, news, weather, or whatever notification has sounded on your phone.

- When you're talking on the phone and another call comes in, allow it to go to voicemail. The person you're talking to now should have your attention. The other person can wait.

- Turn off the television and other devices in your bedroom and turn your attention towards each other.

- Create "no cell phone" zones in your house, including the dinner table, your bed, during family time, on date night, and on vacation.

- Keep cell phone use hands free while driving.

Technology doesn't have to be a bad thing. In fact, when used intentionally, you can make it serve your marriage. For example, we share a calendar. All of our personal and professional commitments are in one place, and each of us can easily access it at any time. There are apps that allow you to share your to-do lists, grocery lists, and banking and budgeting responsibilities. There are even apps designed to help you document or grow your relationship. Used within reason, social media can be a place to celebrate your marriage and share your love for your lifemate and your family. And of course, technology allows you to stay in touch more than ever. Even if you have to leave your cell phone in a locker when you go to work, you can always text your spouse a love note during your lunch break. Discipline yourself to make technology work for you, not against you. Choose to use it productively, in service of your life goals and your marriage, and limit its ability to be a force for destruction.

FOCUS ON THE MOST IMPORTANT THINGS

When Robin and Greg's young child was diagnosed with a serious illness that required out-of-state medical care, the couple sat down and discussed how they would handle it. For a period of time, their son's medical care would be the number one priority in their lives. Robin, a homemaker, would be the one to travel with him. Greg, who was serving in the Air Force, would need to manage things at home while she was gone. They were in agreement that, for the time being, their marriage would take a back seat to their son's treatment. Because they had a strong relationship and a clear vision for what life would look like during and after the treatment, they were able to survive the kind of challenge under which many marriages break.

Unlike Robin and Greg, many people go through life without thinking about their priorities. In the military, you understand your mission priorities and the related daily tasks. At any given moment, you know what the most important and urgent thing is. We've developed a simple framework that makes it easy for you to always know what the most important and urgent thing is in your life too. Here's what that framework of priorities looks like:

First: your relationship with God

Second: your relationship with your spouse

Third: your relationship with, and the raising of, your children

Fourth: your extended family, including parents, siblings, and others

Fifth: your work, career, and workplace relationships

Sixth: all extracurricular activities, including hobbies, volunteer work, and church ministries

This framework is designed to be flexible because there are times when your priorities will need to temporarily shift. A sick child may need to take priority over your marriage until he or she is well. An elderly parent may require a significant amount of your attention for a specific period of time. Training for your job may require you to hand off some of your family responsibilities to your lifemate. Once those situations are resolved, the framework provides a clear order for how things should fall back into place.

Notice that we place your church activities in the very last slot. It's good to be of service to God's people, but we all know that person who's a greeter, a deacon, on the men's ministry, serving on the senior citizens' committee, teaching Bible study, and at church five or six nights a week. (In fact, you or your lifemate might just be that person.) Before you know it, all his time and energy are sucked up by the church. He no longer has time for his wife and kids. His priorities get completely out of whack, and his marriage and family suffer. When you follow the framework and discipline yourself to always return to it when things shift, you don't have to worry about this happening to you.

MAKE THE MOST OF YOUR TIME

When our kids were small, I (Myra) really had to organize and prioritize my day to make the most of my time. If you let them, babies and small children will take up all of your time. I often got up early in the morning to clean the house, so by the time the kids were awake, I could have breakfast with them and spend time focused on family. By dinner time, I had taken care of the other areas of my life so I could focus on the evening meal and give the family my attention again.

You want to get the most out of every area of your life, including your work, marriage, family, health and fitness, and continual self-improvement. Take work for example. You work to make a living, but also to advance your career and grow professionally. One of the best ways to do that is to take time to plan before you begin your day. If you dedicate one percent of your time each day, just fourteen minutes, to think about what you want to accomplish and how you'll do it, you'll find you're able to get the most important things done more efficiently. Do this for your job, and do this for your marriage, and you'll be well ahead of most of your peers.

Experts like Stephen Covey, author of *The 7 Habits of Highly Effective People* and other books, talk about taking care of the boulders first. Taking care of the small things can make you feel like you're being productive when, in reality, nothing important is getting done. Prioritize the things that can make a big difference in each area of your life—these are the boulders—and then discipline yourself to handle those before you get caught up in the minutiae of the day. It also helps to understand the way your energy and creativity fluctuate throughout the day. I (Michael) am most creative in the mornings, so that's when I take care of the big boulders in my day. I save the afternoons for small things that don't require as much focus, creativity, or mental energy.

Whatever you're focused on, be present to that activity in the moment. If you're spending time with your kids, make the most of it by giving them your full attention, listening to what they have to say, and creating memories you can all share. When you're at work, give your job one hundred percent effort. The same applies to every important area in your life. The discipline required to continually be present and make the most of your time will help you become a more self-disciplined person and a better lifemate.

FOCUS ON IMPROVING YOUR GIFTS

As a kid, I (Michael) always knew I wanted to run. I always came in first or second in my elementary school races, and I enjoyed it. When I got older and joined the track team, I told my coach I wanted to be a sprinter. Those were the cool guys. But the coach sent me over to run with the middle-distance runners. Still, I practiced with the sprinters and managed to have myself put in the 100-meter race in my first meet. The gun went off, and those boys took off, leaving me behind like the tortoise watching a bunch of hares cross the finish line. At the next practice, I walked across the track to train with the middle-distance guys. I had identified my gift for running, but the coach had better insight into my real abilities. In adulthood, I've channeled that gift into running long distance, including six marathons to date.

We all have gifts placed in us by God. Sometimes they become lifelong recreational pursuits, like running has been for me. Sometimes they become practical skills you use every day, like cooking. In other cases, those gifts become the foundation for building a business or finding the perfect career. Whether your gifts play a small role in your life or a big one, you can develop your capacity for self-discipline by consistently working to improve them. If you're a runner, follow a training schedule to prepare for a race. If you're a baker, you can take a class and challenge yourself to bake more complicated recipes. You can improve your skills in painting, gardening, coding, singing, writing, design, speaking—wherever your natural gifts are found.

If you're not sure what your gifts are, it's easy enough to figure it out. What kinds of things interest you now or interested you when you were younger? What do you enjoy doing with your free time? What topics do you like to read books about? What do other people think of when they think of you? You don't have to be the best in the world at it. You just have to be passionate about it and willing to find where you fit in that niche. Something as seemingly ordinary as being great at getting people to like and share your social media posts could lead to a side gig or a full-blown business in social media management. Something as commonplace as a love of music could turn out to be the key to your gift. Experiment until you find something you like enough to stick with for a while.

When you're constantly striving to get better at what you do well, you will improve the gifts you were blessed with, and you'll naturally become more self-disciplined. It takes consistency, practice, and a willingness to grow and change to develop your gifts. Those traits exercised in one area will naturally spill over into other areas of your life. Disciplining yourself to get to the next level with your gifts will help you become a more self-disciplined person overall.

DO WHAT FEELS RIGHT, NOT JUST WHAT FEELS GOOD

Carlos worked hard all day, so when he came home in the evenings, he went almost immediately to the den, picked up the video game controller, and stayed there on the couch for hours. Rather than interact with his wife, Amanda, or help her get dinner ready and make sure the kids were taken care of, he fell into the fantasy world of his favorite video games. He took his dinner into the den to eat while he played his games, and when Amanda went to bed at night, she was alone because her husband was still wrapped up in his games.

Carlos convinced himself there was nothing wrong with spending his entire evening alone and leaving his wife on her own. He saw this as a way to decompress at the end of the work day, but in reality, it was a way to escape his real life and he'd become addicted to the games. Amanda, who looked forward to seeing him at the end of each day, felt abandoned. After some coaching, Carlos came to terms with the fact that his wife needed more of his time, and he committed to skipping the games and giving her his attention a few nights a week. He realized it was better for his wife, his marriage, and in the long run, for him, to choose what felt right over what felt good.

The video games felt good to Carlos in the moment. They took his mind off all the realities of work and family obligations. However, those hours spent playing games were costing him a price he didn't even know he was paying. Had he continued down that path, video games might not have cost him his marriage, but they would've almost certainly cost him the ability to have a *strong, happy* marriage.

Author and motivational speaker Jim Rohn said, "Everyone must choose one of two pains: the pain of discipline or the pain of regret." Do you do what feels good in the moment, even if it's the wrong thing to do, only to have regrets later? Or do you choose what feels difficult or even unpleasant in the moment because it's the right thing to do? Doing what feels good in the short-term can provide immediate satisfaction, but the long-term consequences might be disastrous. In those moments of decision, project where each choice will take you and your marriage in the coming days, weeks, and years. Choosing to do what feels right can have tremendous positive benefits, including the satisfaction of being a person of integrity. Choosing what feels good in the moment can have tremendous negative consequences. It may cost you your self-respect, your reputation in your lifemate's eyes, or even your marriage and your relationship with your children.

Becoming more self-disciplined is a strategy to protect and nurture your marriage. Without that discipline, it's difficult, if not impossible, to be a man or woman of integrity, the kind of person who has his or her priorities in order and consistently honors his or her wedding vows. However, when you choose to take ownership of your destiny and the fate of your marriage by becoming disciplined in the way you live and the way you love, you greatly increase your chances of having a happy, healthy, successful military marriage.

Create Your LifeM8Z Moment

Think about your responses to each question or prompt individually, and then turn to each other and thoughtfully share your responses.

1. In what aspects of my life am I self-disciplined?

2. Am I determining my path through life, or am I being flung to and fro like I'm at the wrong end of a whip?

3. Search your heart and identify three to five areas of your character that you need to reinforce to make yourself a person of integrity.

4. List five ways you can use your computer or cell phone to maintain a strong connection with your spouse when you are deployed or away on temporary duty.

5. Make a commitment to each other that you will only use technology and social media to remain faithful and maintain contact with each other.

CHAPTER 5

Are You Ready to Love and Be Loved?

Shonda was an attractive young lady, but when she and her husband, Isaiah, came to us for marriage coaching, something else stood out even more than her beauty. Shonda had built a wall around her heart. In our sessions, she was so stoic that we came to think of her as the Ice Queen. While very little was happening on the surface, we could see she had a lot going on inside. Shonda experienced the same range of feelings as any warm-blooded woman; she just didn't allow anyone, not even Isaiah, to see them. She'd walled off her heart to protect herself from any kind of vulnerability, but it also kept her from loving to the max. Without vulnerability, she couldn't show her husband who she really was. She couldn't fulfill her marriage mission—to ensure her lifemate's needs were met.

Isaiah made it clear that he loved his wife and wanted their marriage to work. Shonda insisted she was also committed to the relationship, but it was clear she was conflicted. She wanted to return her husband's love, but she was afraid to open up. Shonda didn't trust that her husband's love was real, so she did what she could to test him and prove that he'd eventually give up on the marriage. She didn't have a job at the time, but she'd get up in the morning, dress impeccably, and go out for the day. She was secretive about how she spent her time because she wanted her husband to wonder if she was cheating. On one hand, she wanted Isaiah to prove he'd love her no matter what. On the other hand, she wanted him to prove her right and finally abandon her.

Shonda really wasn't ready to love her husband or to openly accept his love for her. She didn't trust herself to be happy in her marriage. She didn't trust that her husband loved her the way he said he did, and without knowing it, she did her best to sabotage the marriage. We are not licensed psychological counselors or therapists, so we don't do a deep dive into our clients' past or any trauma they may have experienced. Marriage coaching is much more focused on the present and the future, but after years of working with hundreds of couples in private coaching and in workshops and seminars, we easily recognize certain patterns of behavior. To us, it appeared that Shonda was allowing the hurt from a previous relationship to interfere with her marriage.

GHOSTS OF PAST RELATIONSHIPS

Any betrayal or disappointment you've experienced in the past can negatively affect your marriage if you let it. It doesn't matter if your former spouse or partner stole your money, ruined your credit, physically or mentally abused you, lied to you, or cheated on you. Any kind of broken trust can leave you bitter or unreasonably suspicious, and if you enter into marriage in those states, your lifemate will usually pay the price. If we had to guess, we'd say a failed relationship in her past had left Shonda unwilling to trust. She really loved Isaiah, but she refused to open up to him.

It was like she was driving down the road with one foot on the accelerator and the other on the brake. Shonda was propelled toward love, happiness, and connection—all things she really wanted—but the brakes were stopping her from getting there. In her case, the brakes were thoughts like, *I'm not worth it, he's not worth it*, and *he's just going to hurt me eventually*. Those kinds of thoughts are learned. Either you take them on from your family, community, or culture, or you learn them in failed romantic relationships. These ghosts of past relationships can wreak havoc on a marriage.

Under similar circumstances, many couples quit too soon. They think the marriage itself must have been a mistake, and they look for a way out. Fortunately, Isaiah and Shonda both had the maturity to recognize something was wrong and to seek expert help. They opted for marriage coaching with us. As coaches, we elected to treat Shonda with kid gloves and not push her too hard because, after all, ice queens are fragile. She needed time to shift her thinking and begin to see that Isaiah had no responsibility for what she'd gone through in the past. Isaiah also needed to understand that his wife wasn't reacting to anything he'd done and that she needed his continued patience, compassion, and support. To facilitate those changes, we gave the couple the tools to step into each other's worlds and see each other's different perspectives without getting defensive, starting with the hand-in-hand, eye-to-eye, knee-to-knee communication process.

As they went through marriage coaching, both spouses actively participated in the exercises we shared with them. Shonda slowly opened up and allowed herself, little by little, to be more vulnerable. Isaiah continued to show up for his wife. He did his best to demonstrate that he would be there for her no matter what, and his perseverance eventually paid off. When we ran into them a couple of years later, Shonda looked like a completely different woman. She was warm and loving toward Isaiah. The Ice Queen was dead, and their marriage was flourishing.

When we talk about the ghosts of past relationships, we often focus on adultery because it's one of the most common issues we see in our coaching, seminars, and workshops. However, infidelity isn't the only past betrayal that can haunt your new relationship.

Ghosts of past relationships include:

- Infidelity
- Lack of intimacy
- Abandonment
- Physical abuse
- Mental and verbal abuse

- Financial exploitation
- Lying and secret-keeping
- Any behavior that leaves you mistrustful or hardened

THE LASTING IMPACT OF INFIDELITY

No one is surprised that infidelity can create tormenting memories in the spouse who suffered on the receiving end of that breach of trust. However, we often overlook the fact that infidelity also hurts the people who participate in it, and these effects can last long after the affair ends. When our client Richard was single, he committed multiple infidelities with different married women. One day, Richard noticed an attractive woman in the base gym. He approached her and introduced himself. Like Richard, Iris was active duty, and they discovered they were assigned to the same unit. The two talked, exchanged numbers, and soon started dating. Richard fell in love for the first time, and within a year, he and Iris were married. According to Richard, the first three months of the marriage were amazing, but things went downhill fast.

Richard noticed other men flirting (his word, not ours) with his wife. He felt himself growing jealous, which strained his relationship with Iris. Instead of focusing on the best parts of his marriage, Richard grew more suspicious about his wife's activities, his mistrust fueled by memories of his own experience. "If those married women were willing to cheat on their husbands with me," he reasoned to himself, "then maybe Iris is capable of doing the same thing to me." Richard was tapped to deploy to the Middle East, and for the entire tour, he obsessed over what Iris was doing without him there to watch her movements and question her. He felt sure some man had come along and enticed her to do the same thing he'd convinced other married women to do with him. Fear is sometimes defined as "false evidence appearing real." For Richard, this was the case. He projected his insecurities and past poor choices on his wife. His fear created a reality in his mind that didn't exist in the real world.

From Iris's point of view, Richard's suspicions were completely unfair. Imagine constantly being accused of something you haven't done and have no intention of doing. It's like being convicted until you're proven to be guilty. It's a hard row to hoe when there's no trust, whether the loss of confidence is justified or not. No matter what Iris did, Richard would twist the truth to fit the reality he created in his mind. It was like he had a little devil on one shoulder and a little angel on the other. Instead of listening to the angel's pleas for him to trust his wife, Richard was transfixed by the powerful messages the little devil continually fed him.

It took months, but we were able to help Richard realize the danger his incessant, undeserved mistrust posed to their marriage. Eventually, Richard realized the little devil he'd been listening to was able to influence him because his own misperceptions of Iris's behaviors fed the devil and made it more powerful. Gradually, Richard learned that trust is a critical foundational element of successful relationships, and without trust, their marriage would be doomed. Both Richard and Iris accepted their mission to do the hard work and the heart work as a cohesive team in order to transform their marriage by fighting to create an atmosphere of trust. Here are a few lessons they learned:

1. Practice hand-in-hand, eye-to-eye, knee-to-knee communication to give your lifemate your undivided attention and ensure you see, feel, and hear each other.

2. Make honesty a part of who you are, and be 100 percent transparent, telling the whole truth and nothing but the truth and trusting in each other to avoid even little white lies.

3. Commit to a strict discipline of talking about and addressing everything, leaving nothing off limits.

4. Affirm your love and your commitment to each other and to your marriage every day.

5. We build trust one brick at a time, over time, but we can destroy that trust in a fraction of a second because of one irresponsible and catastrophic indiscretion. Richard and Iris learned that it takes a long time to build trust and it takes an even longer time to rebuild it. They agreed to avoid doing anything that could jeopardize the newly built trust between them.

RECOVERING FROM ABUSIVE RELATIONSHIPS

We also see cases in which previous abusive relationships negatively affect current marriages. Too often, one or both spouses get caught up in a pattern of abuse. Women who were abused in one relationship may attract the same kind of man in the next relationship. Sometimes husband and wife are violent with each other. We've coached female clients who never thought they could be violent, but the tension and volatility in their marriage drove them to the point of war and they took a swing or threw something at their husband. One or both ended up getting arrested, and had they caused more serious harm, they could've done real jail time. Still, the damage was done. Information about misconduct by the military member or their dependents often makes its way to the military police blotter, gaining the ultimate attention of the unit commander.

Whether the abuse is physical or mental, you never have to live in an abusive relationship. In the case of physical abuse, it's essential that you remove yourself from the situation at least until you can get some help. If the military member is the abuser, their actions may result in directed counseling, non-judicial punishment, court-martial, confinement, or being kicked out of the military. If you are the victim of physical abuse, getting distance from your abuser could mean the difference between life and death. The National Domestic Violence Hotline offers help for victims, survivors, and abusive partners. You can contact the hotline at 1-800-799-7233 or 1-800-787-3224 (TTY). You can also live chat with an advocate at thehotline.org.

Getting completely out of an abusive relationship should be the end of it, but too often the ghosts of that past troubled relationship follow you to your new marriage. Be careful not to project the behavior of your former spouse or partner on your current lifemate. It's unfair, and it will harm your marriage. You may need therapy, counseling, or coaching to move past the pain of the failed relationship, but your marriage is worth the investment of time and effort. If your lifemate is struggling to trust you because of past abuse, be patient and understanding, and seek professional help together.

GET READY TO LOVE

Are you ready to love and to be loved? In order to know for sure, you have to do a serious self-assessment. If you've been in a serious relationship in the past, start by reflecting on what went right and what went wrong.

Ask yourself:

1. What were my needs in that relationship?
2. Which of my needs were met?
3. Which of my needs went unmet?
4. What were my partner's needs?
5. Which of those needs did I leave unmet, and why?

6. What led to the breakup of that relationship, and what part did I play?

7. If there was cheating or betrayal of some kind, what part did I play in that?

8. What did I do right?

9. What did I do wrong?

10. What should I have done more of?

11. What should I have done less of?

12. What could I have done better?

13. Did I do everything within my power to make it work?

14. Did I sabotage the relationship?

15. Did I go into the relationship with an open heart and mind?

Once you've answered those questions, we suggest you perform a SWOT (Strengths, Weaknesses, Opportunities, and Threats) analysis of your current marriage. This technique was initially developed for organizational strategic planning, but it's also incredibly effective in marriages too. The analysis is very simple. Working together, make a list of the strengths, weaknesses, opportunities, and threats in your marriage. Discuss how the two of you are a stronger, more effective team when you unify your strengths, improve your weaknesses, take advantage of opportunities, and neutralize any threats.

We believe there's a simple way to drastically reduce the divorce rate in the military and in this country. If every man and woman became more intentional and persistent in joyfully meeting their lifemate's needs, the rate of divorce would drop dramatically. In the military, we're always focused on the mission, and the mission of marriage is to make sure your lifemate's needs are met. Because of the unique stressors of military life, we have to double and triple our efforts to make sure we successfully carry out that marriage mission. We have to work harder to stay connected, especially when we're hundreds or thousands of miles away from our lifemate. Openness, honesty, transparency, and effort are even more important for us than they are in civilian marriages.

We suggest you write a mission statement that's unique to your marriage. Independently answer the following questions to create your marriage mission statement:

1. Where do we see ourselves in the next three, five, and fifteen years?

2. What do I need to do to achieve those goals?

3. What do I need to change to achieve those goals?

4. What do I need to measure to ensure the goals are met?

Share your answers with your spouse and merge them to create a joint marriage mission statement and plan for where you want to be, how you're going to get there, and how you're progressing to the completion of that mission.

ELIMINATE THE IMPOSSIBLE STANDARD OF PERFECTION

Think about how you would describe the perfect wife or the perfect husband. Women, do you see a man who drives a Bentley, has six-pack abs, and pays for everything even if you make a good living for yourself? He can't have any kids from previous relationships, even if you do. Men, maybe you envision the perfect wife as a beautiful, well-mannered lady in the street who has a dancer pole in your bedroom and knows how to use it. She makes plenty of money, prepares meals from scratch, and swings around that pole for you every night. Or maybe you don't want any of that in your ideal lifemate. Maybe you imagine something completely different, but if it isn't who your lifemate already is, you need to stop imagining and start embracing reality. Whatever your image of the perfect husband or wife is, take a hard look at it. Understand where the image came from and lovingly accept the fact that your lifemate will never be perfect (and neither will you).

Proverbs 18:22 (NKJV) says, "He who finds a wife finds a good thing, and obtains favor from the Lord." It doesn't say anything about finding a perfect wife (or husband). None of us come into the world looking for perfection in a mate. Your early influences, like your parents and other relatives or the TV shows and movies you watch as a kid and as a young adult, shape your initial ideas of what marriage should look like and what qualities your lifemate should have. Some of that is for the good and some isn't, but in recent decades, the media influence on how we view marriage has grown exponentially. For many of us, that influence is a nearly constant presence. The constant exposure to unrealistic standards comes from reality shows, music videos, movies, and social media stars who present extreme and unattainable images.

The media influence is pervasive, but most couples are unaware of how those images affect their marriage. When you're constantly bombarded with visuals of how life is supposed to be, it's easy to take on those ideas as your own. You don't fit the image yourself, but the media can convince you that your spouse should meet those impossible standards. Just like the explosion of wedding shows and reality TV weddings led many people to think a nice wedding has to cost tens or hundreds of thousands of dollars, media does its best to convince us that perfect people, marriages, and lives actually exist. Nothing could be further from the truth, and expecting perfection (something you don't have to give in return) from your lifemate can destroy your marriage. Seek healthier, more realistic images of marriage. Early in our marriage, we found that model in Dan and Gwen White, and we've shared their story and their example with many other couples. Keep looking until you find the mentors or role models who can help you build a healthy, happy marriage.

We sat on a panel for a single's ministry, and a woman stood up and asked, "How do you find your ideal man?" She explained that she was looking for a man who was six-feet tall, drove a BMW, had a nice body, and made a specific amount of money. Her list went on and on. If you have that kind of list, we suggest you print it out on a piece of paper, set it on fire, and watch it go up in smoke. What you want and what God has in store for you may be completely different. If you're busy looking for what's on your list, you may very well miss the mate God designed for you.

Expecting perfection can also show up in small ways. I (Michael) have a major pet peeve: dishes in the sink. Even if the plates and silverware are rinsed clean, I don't want to see them in the sink. I want them in the dishwasher. My wife is a little different. She might have a cup of tea and leave the empty cup next to the sink. She's planning to use it again, but before she can boil more water, I've come behind her and moved the cup to the dishwasher. Not having dishes in the sink is my preference, not hers. To expect her to do things my way, keep the sink empty at all times, and always load the dishwasher exactly the way I want would be completely unreasonable. If there's something you like done a certain way, then you need to do it yourself and not be overly controlling or expect your lifemate to conform to your wishes in every little thing.

Of course, it's okay to make some requests of your lifemate, but don't expect anyone to honor all of your requests to the letter. Fifteen years ago, when Myra and I attended one of our first marriage enrichment seminars, we participated in a facilitated exercise in which we shared three things we found attractive about our mate and three things our mate did that annoyed us. Describing what we found attractive about each other was easy, but I was astounded when Myra disclosed how annoyed she was by my habit of scraping the fork across my teeth when I ate. I was shocked to realize she'd been sitting across the table from me for more than twenty years, cringing with every bite I took. It wasn't a big thing, and I was able to handle her precious feedback and do my best to stop the behavior that annoyed her. Myra didn't expect me to be perfect, but making that small change was an easy way for me to contribute to her happiness.

There's a line in the movie *Good Will Hunting* that sums up the search for the perfect mate: "You're not perfect, sport, and let me save you the suspense. This girl you've met, she's not perfect either. But the question is whether or not you're perfect for each other." Don't make the mistake of searching for Mr. or Ms. Perfect. There's no such thing as a perfect woman or a perfect man. We have family friends who many people find to be an odd couple. She's close to six-feet tall, and he's just at about five-foot-five. She towers over him in pictures and as they walk down the street. If you'd asked her in high school, it's highly unlikely she would've said she had her heart set on a short man. But here's the thing: he's a wonderful husband. They're perfect for each other, and they're very happy together. On the other hand, there are plenty of Hollywood stars who might fit your superficial list, but they have no capacity to maintain a loving, stable marriage. Endeavor to develop the discernment to recognize your perfect partner, the ability to open your heart, and the self-awareness to prepare yourself to be ready to love the right person.

Because naval vessels (like destroyers, guided missile cruisers, and aircraft carriers) spend a lot of time in the water, sea life attaches to the hulls of those vessels over time. Periodically, divers go down and scrape off the moss and barnacles that can negatively impact the performance of the ship. For maximum efficiency, all of that has to be cleared away. The same holds true for us. Throughout our lives, we pick up stuff that slows us down and warps our thinking. You can't reach perfection, but you can strive to be the best possible version of you. Make the decision to do some spring cleaning, deal with your issues, and free yourself to live your best life. Let go of past pains and hurts, release unobtainable expectations of perfection, and get ready to love hard and without restriction.

A HEALTHY MARRIAGE—TRULY READY TO LOVE

Many of the couples we coach come from single-parent households. Some were raised by a grandmother or an aunt with no male figure in the home. They have no close, personal example of a strong, loving, healthy, and happy marriage. Often, they'll refer to TV shows like *The Cosby Show* and the more current *Black-ish* as their best examples of a solid marriage. While we appreciate the occasional positive imagery on TV, that's still not real life. You and your spouse are not Heathcliff and Clair Huxtable. As much as we appreciate the messages of that show, Dr. and Mrs. Huxtable never fought and had very few real challenges to their marriage. They don't represent an example anyone can actually live up to in the real world.

What does a healthy marriage look like? When both partners are truly ready to love, you will know this by the fruit of the marriage. It should mirror the fruit of the Spirit from Galatians 5:22-23:

- Love
- Joy
- Peace
- Patience
- Kindness
- Goodness
- Faithfulness
- Gentleness
- Self-control

Is this fruit manifested in your marriage? Is it reflected in you and the way you treat your lifemate? If not, you have the ability to change that. The fruit of the Spirit in a marriage comes from each lifemate nurturing the fruit of the Spirit in him or herself and in their marriage. Your personal spiritual development is essential to your ability to give and receive love. Allowing yourself to fully love again requires you to make a simple decision. Decide to forgive your current or former mate, forgive yourself, and let go of anything that's holding you back from the future you deserve. Consider it a form of exorcism to drive away any lingering ghosts of the past that are crippling your love life.

As Christians, we're taught that if we are remorseful, we're committed to changing our ways, and we confess, we are forgiven. However, Matthew 6:14-15 (NKJV) also says, "For if you forgive men their trespasses, your heavenly Father will also forgive you. But if you do not forgive men their trespasses, neither will your Father forgive your trespasses." Forgiveness isn't just something you receive. It's something you also have to give. It's easy to say, but in practice, even if we've asked for forgiveness, we may continue to hold on to past hurts, regrets, and guilt. You can't ever know if the person who hurt you is truly remorseful or not, and he or she may never confess. You forgive them not for their sake, but for your sake and for the sake of your marriage.

Deciding to love again after a painful and disheartening divorce or breakup can be difficult. The pain, disappointment, betrayal, and distrust can cause you to build a wall around your heart in an attempt to never be hurt again. However, the wall you build to protect and safeguard yourself also blocks others, including your lifemate, from connecting with you. The longer you allow this wall to stay up, the more you mistakenly come to depend on this barrier and fortification as a safe place. A walled-in heart will find itself searching unsuccessfully for love, again and again. Every relationship it finds will be derailed by self-sabotage. You will never enjoy love, joy, and peace until you confront, resolve, and release those past hurts. To move on in life and love, you have to see the wall for what it is—an impenetrable sanctuary that not only fends off the possibility of future hurts, but is also a prison of your own making that keeps you locked inside, shackled, and lonely.

You will know you're ready to love and to be loved when you feel worthy and deserving of love and you're willing to be open and vulnerable with your lifemate. You're ready to love when you're willing to do the work to improve yourself for the sake of your marriage and when you see the fruit of the Spirit coming to life in your relationship. When you can release past hurts, forgive your ex-partner or even your current partner for the pain he or she caused you, and when you're willing to own responsibility for the part you played in those events, you're ready to love.

Create Your LifeM8Z Moment

Think about your responses to each question or prompt individually, and then turn to each other and thoughtfully share your responses.

1. Have you allowed ghosts of past relationships to influence your marriage? If so, discuss them with your mate and develop a strategy to expel them.

2. Do you commit time to assessing and discussing the health of your marriage?

3. Do you have a history of allowing friends and family to block you from the love you deserve?

4. Do you struggle with ex-romantic relationships interfering with your current relationship?

5. Make two lists: 1) five things you love, respect, and cherish about yourself, and 2) five things you love, respect, and cherish about your mate.

CHAPTER 6

Set Boundaries, Prune Past Relationships, and Survive Deployments

Chelsea and Patrick, an attractive couple, had both served in the military and had both been deployed. Unfortunately, they'd also both had affairs, leaving their marriage on rocky ground. They were remorseful about it and trying to deal with it, but they weren't on the best terms and hadn't made much progress when Patrick was tapped to deploy again. Chelsea, who had gotten out of the military by then, tried to call and FaceTime her husband at their scheduled times, but he missed a couple of those dates. Naturally, Chelsea became suspicious. If he wasn't available, who was he with? Sometimes, when Patrick did answer, she heard conversations and female laughter in the background. She knew women were an integral part of Patrick's unit and they deployed alongside the men, but her mind raced with the possibility that her husband was cheating again.

The disappointment and distrust worked both ways. More than once, Patrick called home at their prearranged time, and Chelsea didn't answer. It didn't take long for him to start to wonder if she was spending time with some other man. For another couple, a few missed calls might've been easily explained, but for them, it brought up all the old hurt they each felt from the other's past betrayal. Ultimately, Patrick stepped outside of the marriage while he was overseas, and Chelsea, a beautiful woman with lots of guys hitting on her, ended up surrendering to that same temptation.

As angry, disappointed, and frustrated as they were with each other, Patrick and Chelsea still wanted to fight for their marriage. When Patrick returned, they decided to get some help figuring out how to rebuild trust and honor their vows. They wanted coaching from a couple who could see things from both the husband's and the wife's point of view, and they were looking for someone who understood what it was like to deal with the challenges of military life. They called us.

Through coaching, we were able to help the couple see where their marriage had gotten derailed. They accepted that marriage requires hard work and heart work, and they believed it would be worth it. They employed strategies to rebuild the trust they'd lost, including overserving each other, being transparent about what was going on in their lives when they were separated, and answering each other's questions without getting defensive. Patrick and Chelsea recommitted to their marriage mission and were able to save the relationship.

As Chelsea and Patrick discovered, marriage doesn't come with instructions, op orders, or roadmaps. After you say, "I do," you're tossed out there to figure it out on your own, and that doesn't always work out well. Don't wait until your marriage is struggling to get support. Instead, get a mentor or coach as soon as you can. If you can get that kind of guidance early in your marriage, you'll have a better chance of avoiding some of the common traps couples fall into. As a military husband and wife, learning from the proven experience of a more experienced, solid military couple can be a great way to learn how to handle deployments and come out stronger.

Deuteronomy 24:5 (NIV) tells us, "If a man has recently married, he must not be sent to war or have any other duty laid on him. For one year he is to be free to stay at home and bring happiness to the wife he has married." As modern military members, you won't always have the option to spend a year with your spouse before you're deployed, but the message of that verse is clear. It's important to invest in your marriage when you're together. Nurturing your relationship while you're under the same roof will make it so much easier for your marriage to survive when you're apart.

ACCEPTING THE REALITY OF DEPLOYMENT

Every branch of the military has deployment down to a science. Pre-deployment actions, like immunizations, preparing a will, and renewing ID cards, are spelled out to make sure both the military member and his or her family are set up for success. Military members receive thorough training about potential threats and cultural norms, things to do and not to do, and everything necessary to prepare for deployment. The military member also receives assistance in setting up his or her spouse to handle things on the home front. Non-military members attend seminars about what the military members may experience. They can tap into a variety of resources, like the base chapel, unit support groups, spouse luncheons, childcare, and family activities, to make the deployment experience a little easier. However, the only way to truly understand deployment from either the side of the military member or the family left behind is to go through it.

Deployments can last a week, a month, many months, or longer. (Some military members deployed to Afghanistan for a year and did multiple tours.) Once the units are tasked and begin their spin-up for operational deployment, the military member and his or her family are affected by the increased battle rhythm as they prepare for possible military action. Every military family has to face a moment of realization as deployment approaches. There's a possibility that this military member could end up making the ultimate sacrifice. Many young people come into the military because they want a good job and a solid profession. But when they get tapped to go over to Kuwait or Afghanistan for six months, all of a sudden, things get real. As the professional citizen-warriors they are, they will salute smartly and go wherever they are called. But the first time your spouse is called up, the serious risks they face start to sink in. As a young captain going through Squadron Officer School, I (Michael) listened to former POWs and people who'd been severely wounded in combat share their experiences, and it opened my eyes to what we, as members of the military, put on the line.

During the Vietnam War, my father experienced that risk firsthand. He was stationed at Cam Ranh Bay, in Vietnam, and amazingly, he discovered that my mom's brother-in-law, Frank, was stationed there too. The two men had never met stateside, but they became friends at Cam Ranh Bay. One night, the Viet Cong attacked their base. Fuel tanks were blowing up and munitions going off. My dad put on his helmet and sheltered in a type of foxhole. And when he woke up the next morning, he thought, "I'm the only guy left alive." Of course, he wasn't. In fact, one of the first people he saw that morning was Frank, alive and well. He and Frank had made it through the fire, but in one night, the threat of war had become very clear. It's difficult to understand that kind of danger until you face it, but for military members, it's always a possibility.

TAKE ADVANTAGE OF TECHNOLOGY

Because I (Michael) grew up in a military family, I know what it's like for a child to have limited contact with a deployed parent. When my dad was in Vietnam, we wrote letters back and forth. When we wanted to send him a real treat, we'd record a cassette tape. Mom and the three of us kids would all record a message telling Dad what was going on in our lives, and he always looked forward to those tapes. It was a rare opportunity to hear the voices of the family he'd left behind. But a tape is only a one-way communication. Today, technology allows us to see and hear our loved ones no matter how far apart we are. Wi-Fi access might not be perfect where you're deployed, but you'll almost always have some ability to employ technology to stay in touch with your lifemate. Use it.

We coach couples to set strict ground rules for the use of technology in your marriage. Don't argue via text messaging or take jabs at your spouse over Messenger. Don't try to discuss controversial subjects over text message. It's too easy to misinterpret what the other person is saying. Consider technology a way to stay connected, not a tool for working out your deepest problems. Schedule the times when you'll talk and do everything possible to show up and honor that commitment.

HELPING YOUR CHILDREN HANDLE DEPLOYMENT

Families with children have an added level of responsibility when the military member is deployed. Every child is different, and their age, maturity, and level of sensitivity will dictate how you can best guide them through the deployment experience. The oldest of three siblings, I (Michael) was thirteen years old when my dad went to Vietnam. In middle school, I wrote a poem about the war effort, and my teacher asked me, "Do you know somebody over there?" I told her, "Yeah, my dad." She let me know I had her support. That's really what all kids need. A year is a long time for a thirteen-year-old and even longer for younger children, so they need to know the people around them care about what they're going through.

Before my father left, he told me he expected me to help my mom with my younger brother and sister, just two and three years behind me, and be the man of the house. He laughs about it now because I took that charge very seriously. Mom was a civil service secretary, and my siblings and I would beat her home after school. I learned to cook for us, mostly on the disposable grill. I could cook a whole chicken on that grill, and I even made my own barbecue sauce. To this day, I'm still a grill master. I'd never had an inclination to grill before my father deployed, but I saw it as my role to support my mom and comply with my dad's order.

Although I was moving into my teen years when my father left, I still faced some challenges. I watched the news every night and saw the body count for both sides. I watched a lot of the footage—early on in black and white, and later in color—because I was always hoping to catch a glimpse of my dad, alive and well. For whatever reason, once he was deployed, we had to move off base, so it was an odd time for our family. As a kid, I couldn't figure out why we had to move at a time when we most needed the support of our Air Force family.

Because of the move, I transferred from the base junior high to the downtown junior high, where the students and the culture were very different from what I'd known. I stuck out, and the other students talked about me because I dressed differently. One day, I saw a girl I kind of liked, but the student assigned to be my buddy told me, "You don't want to mess with her." When I asked him why, he explained, "She's got a baby." We were only in the seventh grade. I didn't even know how babies were made, and I certainly had never known a thirteen-year-old mother. Your children may not face similar extremes, but they will still need as much support as possible when a parent is deployed.

The realities of war were probably a little more real for me and the other kids who'd been stationed at Dover Air Force Base. The remains of many of the Americans who lost their lives in different wars or military actions return to this country through Dover Air Force Base. It has one of the largest morgues in the world, and even the remains of the Americans who died in the Jonestown massacre came through the base. One day, as I (Michael) drove along with my father on base, I asked him, "What are all those silver boxes on the runway." My dad told me, "Those are caskets." It was a glimpse of the stark reality of military service in times of conflict.

I (Myra) didn't come from a military family, so I came to deployment from the point of view of a wife and mother. While Michael was a young teenager when his father was deployed, our daughter Lindsay was only in second grade when Michael deployed. Her needs and the way she handled her father's absence were very different from a teenager's needs and reactions, and I learned to let the children lead me as to what they needed. How much you choose to talk to your children about the circumstances of their deployed parent will vary based on their age, their personality, and their curiosity and concern. When they have questions, you want to be right there to answer them so that you become their primary source of information. Let them take the lead, and don't force information on them. In our family, the most important thing was to make sure our children received a consistent message from both of us, and especially from me, the parent on the home front, that everything was going to be okay.

Pay attention to changes in your child's behavior when a parent is deployed or away for training or a TDY. Our oldest daughter, Lindsay, would get sick if I (Michael) was away for just a few days. Because Myra recognized the pattern, we were able to address it. Before each departure, I'd sit down with Lindsay and tell her where I was going and when I'd be back and promise to bring her back a souvenir. That conversation helped her manage her expectations and feel secure in the knowledge that Daddy would be coming home.

It's also important to maintain regular communication between children and their deployed parent. Take advantage of technology. Give your children the opportunity to regularly connect and share what's happening at school or in their activities. In most cases, there's no need for a parent to come home to a child who sees him or her as a stranger. The parent-child bond can be kept intact with regular video calls and emails.

SETTING BOUNDARIES TO PROTECT YOUR MARRIAGE

In peacetime, we prepare for war. Setting and living by boundaries in your marriage, well before one or both of you is deployed, will improve your ability to come through deployment with your marriage intact and growing stronger every day. If you live by agreed-upon guidelines while you're both under the same roof, they'll become a habit, and it'll be a lot easier for you to follow them when one of you is thousands of miles away from your lifemate and facing an unusual amount of stress.

Don't assume your lifemate knows what's acceptable to you and what's not, especially when it comes to interactions with the opposite sex. What one of you considers a reasonable boundary may never have occurred to your spouse. For example, I may have a boundary that Myra should never ride alone with a man in his car, but it's my responsibility to communicate that to her and seek agreement. If her car won't start, and a male acquaintance offers her a ride, she might see no reason not to accept the offer. If I haven't told her that's not okay with me, then I can't expect her to read my mind and know it's a concern. There's no point in blowing up at your lifemate over boundaries he or she knew nothing about. Share your thoughts about boundaries and your reasons behind them. Ultimately, any boundaries in the marriage must be agreed upon and followed by both parties, or they won't serve you.

The mission of marriage is to make sure your lifemate's needs are met. Those needs include security and the ability to trust you. If you haven't dealt with issues of infidelity or broken trust in your relationship, you may be thinking this doesn't apply to you, but no marriage is immune to temptation. No matter how much you love each other, you're still human. The separation and trying circumstances that come with deployment can open the door to choices you might otherwise never make, but you can prepare in advance to make sure your marriage doesn't fall victim to infidelity.

Together, you and your lifemate can create rules of engagement to protect your marriage from the threat of outside influences and infidelity before, during, and after deployment. Your rules of engagement will define acceptable behavior for you and your lifemate and your relationships with other members of the opposite sex. They should all be tied back to the marriage mission, not just arbitrary rules.

We suggest you have rules of engagement for the following:

- Social media
- Time alone with the opposite sex
- Friendships with the opposite sex
- Socializing with co-workers
- Consuming alcohol in social situations
- Any areas in which you know you have a weakness

What we share here are general guidelines, but you and your lifemate get to decide what your boundaries will be in each of these areas. Whatever you decide, this is a topic for "us," not "I" and "you." Whatever boundaries you agree on must apply to both of you.

Social media can be used to declare your commitment to each other to the world, or it can be used to tear each other down in front of your friends and family. Don't fight your fights in public. Sharing your arguments on social media is like throwing gasoline on glowing embers. It can cause a small conflict to become a huge blow-up when other people chime in and give their opinions on your marriage. It can also make your marriage look vulnerable, as if one or both of you might be open to entertaining outside relationships. If you need someone to talk to about your disagreements, find a mentor, counselor, or coach to confide in, and keep your private business private.

If one of you is deployed, do *not* announce that on social media. It sends the message that the spouse on the home front is all alone, which can open the door to communications that may seem innocent at first but can quickly turn into trouble for your marriage. That's a slippery slope. A direct message turns into lunch, and lunch turns into a sleepover. Don't put yourself in that situation. You may want the support of your friends and family, but you can go about getting that in other ways. Even if your social media account is private, be aware that your connections can screenshot and share whatever you post. You never know who will see it.

There's never a good reason to have secret social media accounts that your lifemate doesn't know about. That's asking for trouble. Instead, friend and follow each other and share the passwords to your individual accounts. Make it clear that you're both being totally transparent with your social media, and then use those platforms with strategic intention. Use social media to present a united front. Choose profile pictures of the two of you together and make it clear to everyone that your profile is not the place to find a hook-up.

We also minimize our **time alone with members of the opposite sex**. A lot of our clients and potential clients have my phone number, but I (Michael) rarely take a call from a female client without my wife present. If Myra is home, I put the call on speaker so she can participate in the conversation. We keep it professional. This rule of engagement can get complicated if one of you has a child from a previous relationship. In that case, you may have to interact with that co-parent. We haven't experienced that situation, but our rule would be that you don't spend time alone with your ex. If Myra had to pick up a child, I'd want to be there. And if the situation were reversed, I expect that she'd want to be with me when I picked up a child from my ex's house. It sends a strong signal that you've got nothing to hide from your lifemate, and it presents a united front to the ex-spouse or ex-partner so he or she is much less likely to get ideas about interfering in your relationship in any way.

Is it okay for you and your lifemate to have **friends of the opposite sex**? Be specific about how you want to handle this area. You may have opposite-sex friends from before you were married, so you have to decide how those friend-ships need to change. Maybe you'll only hang out with that friend if your lifemate can come along with you, or if your friend is married, you can choose to only go on couples' dates together. We have a female friend who's like a sister to me (Michael). It's fine for Myra and me to stay at her house, but I could only do that if Myra were okay with it. I'm a naturally outgoing and even flirtatious person. Having clear boundaries made it easy for me to keep that behavior in check and make sure it doesn't harm our marriage.

Clearly define what those lines are in your relationship. Is it acceptable for you to have private conversations via text or instant message with your opposite-sex friends? Is it okay for you to have them over to your house without your life-mate present? Address every possible level of interaction. We've seen so many people get themselves in trouble because "innocent" texting turns into sending nude or partially nude pics. It's not innocent, and it can destroy your marriage. Be very clear about what kinds of interactions are acceptable with opposite-sex friends and which are not.

Socializing with co-workers can seem like a natural ex-tension of your work relationships. During the average work day, you likely spend more hours with co-workers than you do with your family, so the opportunity to grow close is al-ways there. Be clear about your boundaries with co-work-ers, especially those of the opposite sex. Being friendly with someone you spend so much time with might seem normal, but what are your limits on that friendliness? A shoulder to cry on, a neck massage in the middle of a long day, or lunch to celebrate a success or commiserate over a tough assignment can mislead an interested co-worker or open the door to temptation.

For the most part, military members have the luxury of leaving our work at work. There's not much need to communicate with co-workers after hours. I (Michael) had disciplined my mind so that I stopped seeing my team members as male or female. It wasn't until we all came to work on a Saturday dressed in our civilian clothes that it struck me that one of the female members of my team was actually a woman. I was so used to seeing her in uniform that it threw me to see her dressed casually with her hair down. I came home and told Myra, "Donna's a woman!" It sounds funny now, but I'd disciplined my mind to see Donna as a Captain, not as male or female. This kind of discipline is particularly useful on deployment, but it is just as important to have rules about whether or not you'll socialize with co-workers after work. If so, when and how will that be appropriate?

Consuming alcohol in social situations can cause inhibitions to drop and judgment to be clouded. Be honest and self-aware about how alcohol affects you. When I (Michael) was out there drinking "two double Bacardi and Cokes, and keep 'em coming," I openly flirted with other women. It hurt my wife, and if I hadn't changed my behavior, it could've cost me my marriage. That young guy who liked to party and drink himself into a coma still lives inside of me. Because I know this about myself, I typically limit my drinking to times when I'm with my wife. When I'm travelling alone, I may have a glass of wine in my hotel room, but you won't find me sitting in the bar, pounding one drink after another. That's a boundary I put on myself to reinforce to my wife that she can trust me.

Your spouse may be able to see how drinking affects your behavior more clearly than you can. If your lifemate shares a concern about your drinking, listen without getting defensive. If you see it in yourself, be adult enough to set appropriate boundaries. If you're really self-aware, you won't wait for your partner to tell you alcohol is putting your marriage at risk. Take the lead, commit to specific limits on when, how much, and with whom you'll drink, and then stick to those limits. Your partner will know if you're being honest or not, so don't bother setting boundaries you have no plans to follow.

Examine any areas in which you know you have a weakness. Alcohol isn't the only weakness that can put your marriage at risk, and only you know what your particular battle is. Be honest with yourself about it and address it long before you face deployment so you can go into that situation with your marriage on the strongest possible foundation. Pornography is a common weakness—for both men and women—that can be destructive to a marriage. If that's a problem in your marriage, deal with it and set and follow boundaries so you can conduct yourself honorably before, during, and after deployment. It may be a battle for you, but it's a battle worth fighting for the sake of your marriage. If you can get a handle on your weaknesses, whatever they are, while you're at home, you'll make it much easier to avoid making bad decisions when you're deployed.

PRUNE POTENTIALLY DANGEROUS RELATIONSHIPS

Our friend Kendra had a close circle of girlfriends. They did lunch and went shopping together, and at least on the surface, she enjoyed their company. One day, one of those friends jokingly said to her, "When your time comes, I'll give you my divorce lawyer's number." In that moment, it hit Kendra that all of her friends in that group were divorced, and they constantly talked about men and marriage with disdain. Divorce was the norm for them. Happy, fulfilling marriages were rare.

Kendra was the only woman in that circle of friends who was still married, and she wanted to stay that way. By her estimation, she and her husband had a wonderful relationship, and she felt uncomfortable with conversations that even jokingly disparaged him. She stopped hanging out with those women because she didn't want their influence to have a negative impact on her marriage. If people in your life are anti-marriage, or even worse, unsupportive of your marriage in particular, they pose a real threat. That's a clear indication and warning for you to fortify your defenses, and if necessary, cut those people loose. Your marriage always needs to be surrounded by people who support it, and this becomes even more important when one of you is deployed.

I (Myra) found out for myself that you have to be careful who you associate with, especially when your lifemate is away. If you leave yourself open to it, you may find yourself surrounded by people with a totally different vision of marriage, people who haven't yet figured out the true mission of marriage. I heard military spouses question whether our military members were really away for work or if they were off having fun and possibly having affairs. It was ridiculous, but if you hear that type of speculation enough, it could impact the way you treat your lifemate when he or she returns. If your marriage doesn't have a strong foundation, or even if you're just having a weak moment, that kind of talk can plant dangerous, destructive suspicions in your mind.

Periodically, look at all of the relationships in your life with a critical eye, and ask yourself, "Have I been entertaining any relationships that aren't one hundred percent conducive to the success of my marriage?" Look closely at who you hang out with at work, who you go to lunch with, who you text, and who you connect with on social media and in other areas of your life. Are you walking the line between friendship and improper relationships? Is there anyone in your life whose view of marriage or opinion of your lifemate might be intentionally or unintentionally harmful to your marriage? Now is the time to be proactive and cut those ties.

Letting go of those relationships is a decision you can make whenever you choose to, and there's no announcement required. You don't need to confront those people or create conflict. Instead, you can simply become unavailable. When our girls were teenagers, we controlled who they could hang around with by making it convenient for them to be around the people we liked but very inconvenient for them to hang around kids we thought were likely to make bad decisions. There was no conflict. Our girls were simply not available. If you decline to go to lunch, hang out after work, or chat on the phone often enough—if you're simply not available— most people will eventually get the message. Even if it feels uncomfortable to say no to someone you used to say yes to, do it. It could make a real difference for your marriage.

COMING HOME

A warm welcome, displays of appreciation, and time alone with their lifemate—those are the immediate needs of most military members returning from deployment. I (Michael) wanted to embrace my children and play with them, and then I wanted someone to watch those kids for the weekend so I could have alone time to reconnect with my wife. That reconnection is even more special when your lifemate takes the time and initiative to set it all up for you. Sexy lingerie, a special dinner, and that special playlist all work together to send the message that you were missed for more than your ability to change the oil or fix the garbage disposal. It allows the two of you to celebrate the fact that you honored your commitment to each other and made it through the deployment before you get back to everyday reality.

When Michael was away from home, I (Myra) had a different life with the girls. They slept in our bed with me, we had breakfast for dinner, and I ran the household a little differently than I did when their father was home. Sometimes, he'd come back and find we'd been waiting on him to fix something around the house, but for the most part we were good. As much as I missed my husband and the girls missed their father, our family continued to function. However, I learned early in our marriage how important it is to make room for the returning spouse. That person needs to have a role and a say-so in how the family is run.

I actually learned that lesson when I was in the hospital for a short while and Michael took care of the girls on his own. When I returned, I questioned the way he did things. I didn't particularly like what he let them wear to school or how he did their hair, and I made a few comments about it. Michael was really hurt by that because he'd done his best and I made him feel like his best was inadequate. The same thing can happen when a military member returns from deployment. He or she wants to step in and be a part of family life again, but it's hard to do that if the spouse on the home front insists on things being done his or her way.

The majority of spouses charged with maintaining the home front do a tremendous job. The women in particular do a great job of supporting each other and living up to the idea that we are a military family. I (Michael) would come back and realize that Myra really did have everything under control. It's easy for a military member to feel irrelevant when it seems like the family did just fine without him or her. However, the spouse on the home front can make that transition home much easier by allowing the returning spouse to resume a leadership role. We military members love a mission, and Myra would give me my standing orders for doing my part to take care of the girls. It allowed me to step right back into my role as their father.

As the spouse managing your home while your lifemate is deployed, you'll likely reorganize the way you do things. Since you're flying solo, you have to do what works best for you, especially if you have children to take care of on your own. Your kids may get used to asking you for permission and doing things that their deployed parent might not allow. However, when your deployed spouse returns, it's important for you both to remember you're a team. Getting back to making decisions together and leading your household as a unit right away will make the transition easier for everyone in the family.

ADDITIONAL SUPPORT FOR RETURNING MILITARY MEMBERS

At a function in Washington, DC, I (Michael) had an exchange with a woman that I'll never forget. When I looked across the table at this First Lieutenant, I couldn't help noticing all the medals on her chest, and one medal in particular stood out. "Excuse me," I said. "Is that a Silver Star?" She confirmed that she had indeed been awarded a Silver Star, one of the highest honors a member of the military can receive. She recounted how the convoy of armored vehicles she was traveling in came under fire and members of her team were injured. She did what she had to do and received the Silver Star for her valor. Her actions were courageous, and she deserved the recognition she received. Sadly, when she returned from her deployment, there was nobody there to meet her and her landlord had boxed up her belongings. She didn't get the welcome home a war hero deserves.

As she told her story, she had a faraway look in her eyes, and I could see that everything she'd gone through was still with her. She didn't share the details of her experience, but she was clearly still haunted by the memories. While the vast majority of military members will tell you it's a high honor to serve, what we do in the military is for real. Sometimes, the impact of what we experience can be lasting and even traumatic.

When a deployed military member returns, any lingering trauma must be addressed, but first, enjoy the reunion for what it is. If you and your lifemate established your Rules of Engagement (ROE) before the deployment, and you've maintained that conduct, congratulate yourselves. As much as you can, share with each other what each of you went through while you were apart. I (Michael) hated going to bed alone. I love my wife, and I missed her, and when I got home, I told her so. Share those kinds of things to reconnect and make it clear that you're glad to be together again. I arranged for a neighbor to watch the kids for the entire weekend when

I returned, and I made sure we didn't have to go out for anything. I pulled down all the shades, and Myra and I had every room of the house available to us and us alone. I was glad I never had the kind of lonely return that First Lieutenant had.

In the days and weeks after your passionate reunion, it's always good to talk with your lifemate, even about any difficulties you experienced. As the home-front spouse, you can support your lifemate by being available and making it easy for him or her to talk about the deployment experience. Words aren't always necessary. Sometimes, the comfort of physical contact is just as important. Physical affection, sitting next to your spouse while you watch TV together and snuggling close in bed, will remind your spouse that you're glad he or she is home and you're there to listen.

Military members may suffer some level of post-traumatic stress disorder (PTSD), and if talking to your lifemate isn't enough, speaking with a mental health professional or a support group of vets who've had similar experiences is always an option. We recognize that it can be difficult to talk about trauma, but with the right support, it is possible. An acquaintance of ours was shot down in Iraq and held as a prisoner of war. His experience was a difficult one, but eventually, he was able to talk about it. For some people, talking about it can make the difference between suffering and recovering.

Sometimes the experience is so traumatic that the military member doesn't want to talk with his or her lifemate about it at all. It's an understandable response but not a healthy one over the long- term. The suicide rate for vets coming back is higher than it should be, and much of that is preventable with proper counseling or treatment. If the military member in your house is struggling to deal with what he or she experienced on deployment, ask for help. Talk to the chaplain, call one of the dedicated hotlines, or join a relevant support group. If you're uncomfortable talking to anyone in the military because you're afraid it could impact your career, you still have options. Find a therapist, counselor, or other mental health professional in private practice who specializes in helping clients deal with PTSD.

Help is always available. To get immediate help for PTSD, please call the Veterans Crisis Hotline at 1-800-273-8255. This support is free, confidential, available 24/7, and serves all veterans and service members, including the National Guard and Reserve, and their family members and friends. In a life-threatening or potentially dangerous emergency related to PTSD, please dial 911 or visit a local emergency room.

THE UPSIDE OF DEPLOYMENT

When you're separated from each other, your marriage changes. There's no getting around that, but whether the change is for the better or for the worse is up to the two of you. You can choose to let deployment cause you to grow closer together or grow distant from each other. If you don't prepare for it, deployment could easily destroy your marriage. On the other hand, if you take on this challenge as a team, pull together, and support each other, you can come out on the other side of deployment with a stronger, happier marriage.

One of the unexpected benefits of deployment is an increase in confidence. You both take on new challenges and can take pride in knowing you've accomplished something most people will never achieve. Let deployment provide an opportunity to reflect on your gratitude for your lifemate and the way the two of you support each other. Surviving deployment with your marriage intact and your family thriving should increase your faith in your relationship and in each other. That kind of success helps you get to the point that you know that you know that you know *that you know* your marriage will make it. Let absence make your heart grow fonder and enjoy the sweet reunions.

Create Your LifeM8Z Moment

Think about your responses to each question or prompt individually, and then turn to each other and thoughtfully share your responses.

1. Discuss with your spouse what behaviors and relationships are in bounds (acceptable) and out of bounds (unacceptable).

2. Agree to immediately terminate any relationship that makes either of you uncomfortable or is perceived as a threat to your marriage. Take turns discussing how to create an atmosphere for your spouse to feel comfortable sharing these concerns.

3. If you are facing a long deployment or family separation, have a family meeting to allow each member to openly share their feelings and fears.

4. Solicit ideas from your spouse and children about how they would like to celebrate the end of a long family separation or deployment.

CHAPTER 7

Accept the LifeM8Z Challenge

Our journey started with a simple, unexpected request. Pastor Benjamin Reynolds of Emmanuel Missionary Baptist Church, in Colorado Springs, Colorado (where Reverend Cleveland A. Thompson is the current senior pastor), approached us one day and asked if we would be interested in starting a marriage ministry. We had been members of the church for a while, and we agreed to take on the assignment. At Focus on the Family, headquartered in North Colorado Springs, a representative provided us with volumes of marriage enrichment material, and with that foundation and a lot of research, we built out a twelve-month marriage ministry curriculum that we were excited to lead. However, we never got the chance to implement it. I (Michael) was promoted from Lieutenant Colonel to Colonel and tapped by the Commanding General to move immediately to Albuquerque, New Mexico, where I became one of the directors at the Air Force Operational Test and Evaluation Center (AFOTEC).

Once Myra and the girls joined me in Albuquerque, we searched for a local church to attend, and someone suggested we try God's House Church. We liked what we saw enough that we joined right away. A couple of weeks later, we were at a bowling event with several other parishioners when Bishop Michael Shelby, the pastor, approached us. "Brother Holmes, Sister Holmes," he said, "my wife and I have been wanting to start a marriage ministry, but we've been too busy. The Lord put it on my heart to talk to you about taking it on." We told Bishop Shelby we could meet with him the next day. We were ready. Pastor Reynolds had planted a seed that his church didn't get to harvest, but our new church home did.

That's how we got started in marriage ministry. The first time we mentored a couple, we had been married for about twenty years, but we were nervous to take on the responsibility. We didn't know what to expect. We certainly didn't expect that experience to lead to years of coaching, mentoring, and teaching thousands of couples how to have a stronger, happier, more passionate marriage, but that's exactly what it turned into. We became vessels for God to speak to those men and women about His plan for marriage. With that purpose in mind, we officially launched LifeM8Z in 2003 to expand our reach.

As Bob Buford describes in *Halftime: Moving from Success to Significance* (Zondervan, 2015), the first half of our life together was about creating success in our work and family, and the second half is about creating significance. We're proud of what we've accomplished in our marriage. We've encountered several storms, but we've made it through, flying high. We've made it through, and our relationship is stronger, better, and more committed. We've reached a point where we both know there's no way either of us will do anything to jeopardize what we've built. We have something special, and we want to share it with as many couples as we possibly can. Our goal is for every marriage (both military and civilian) to be successful.

We're committed to our goal, but we recognize that making a marriage work is hard and that difficulty is compounded for military couples. Enduring the effects of high-pressure jobs, frequent deployments, separations due to duty, and the inherent dangers of military life can take a severe toll on military marriages. Preserving your marriage requires a laser-focused investment of time, energy, resources, and commitment. It's not always easy, but in all but the rarest of cases, it is possible.

Marriage is indeed hard work, but it's also spiritual work. It was the first ministry created by God. Adam and Eve were put together on Earth to worship God and to meet each other's needs. You and your lifemate are designed for the same purposes. God wants you to love Him with all of your heart, soul, and spirit, and He wants you to love your spouse the same way. The two relationships are synergistic. When you grow closer to God, you grow closer to your lifemate, and when you grow closer to your lifemate, you grow closer to God. Your greatest joy in life, apart from pleasing God, should be to please one another. That's what marriage is all about.

The real joy and satisfaction of marriage comes from doing the work. These seven critical skills encompass all the work you need to do to protect and defend your marriage.

1. Know your mission.

April grew up in a close-knit military family. However, when she married Steve, a military member, she still wasn't prepared for the level of commitment required of a military spouse. When Steve received word that his next assignment was overseas, April didn't want to go. She didn't want to leave her big, loving family behind. She wanted their children to grow up with grandparents, aunts and uncles, and cousins nearby. The reality of military life was more complicated and demanding than she'd expected.

When we coached April and Steve, we helped April see that she was now in the same position her parents had once been in. It was her turn to make the adult decisions and support her husband's military career by willingly going where that career took them. It was time to put her marriage in its proper place—just after her relationship with God and before everything else. Once April fully grasped the mission of marriage—to make sure her lifemate's needs were met— things changed for the couple. She made the decision to go where Steve's assignments took them. April took a leap of faith for the sake of their marriage, and the family moved to London. They flourished there. Together, Steve and April built a strong marriage and a strong family.

The mission of marriage is to make sure your lifemate's needs are met. Once you've made the decision to marry, meeting your lifemate's needs becomes your priority. When you see your lifemate as God's gift to you and value him or her accordingly, you naturally want to make sure you're the person taking care of those needs. These aren't boxes you check once or twice. You should spend the rest of your life meeting your lifemate's needs.

Don't make the mistake of getting complacent about this. Remember that complacency is the root of all the problems that crop up in marriage. If you let it, complacency will erode the love, passion, and concern you had for each other when your relationship was new. When you start taking your lifemate for granted, you find excuses not to meet his or her needs. Protect your marriage, and don't let anything distract you from your mission.

2. Get what you want by meeting your lifemate's needs.

Brianna and Kevin loved each other, but they constantly clashed. They often found themselves in violent disagreements, arguing with one another even when they both wanted the same things. Because they had a hard time communicating, they also struggled to meet each other's emotional, intellectual, and physical needs, and neither of them was satisfied in the marriage. They did a lot for each other, but unfortunately, neither of them was doing what the other one really wanted and needed.

When we met with Kevin and Brianna, we helped them to step into each other's worlds so each could see the other's perspective without judgment. It took some time, but as they began to understand each other better, they were able to meet each other's needs. Through this process, they each found their own needs being met more and more of the time, so they no longer had a reason to constantly argue. Their love quotient went up exponentially, and their marriage was transformed.

If you fail to meet your lifemate's needs, you leave the door open for someone or something else to come in and fill the void you've left in your marriage. This could lead to inappropriate friendships, misplaced loyalties, distractions from your marriage, or even infidelity. If, on the other hand, you meet your lifemate's needs, you protect your marriage against interference and you greatly increase your chances of having your own needs met. A fulfilled lifemate is much more likely to be loving, giving, and considerate of your needs.

3. Adopt a winning mindset.

Church life was a top priority for both Jordan and Tanisha. The couple was very religious and took their faith seriously. Before they married, they'd been deeply involved in their church. They each wore at least five different hats at their church home, participating in everything from women's and men's ministries to choir, praise dance, weekly Bible study, and more. After they said, "I do," that commitment to church continued. In fact, their schedules were so filled with church activities that, even though they lived under the same roof, they rarely had time for each other.

When we coached Jordan and Tanisha, we agreed with them that it was important to belong to a Christian community. However, we wanted them to understand that their church activities didn't define their relationships with God. In fact, we saw those activities as extracurricular pursuits, which should come after God, marriage, children, family, and work. With this new priority list in mind, Jordan and Tanisha committed to growing and changing together. Once they agreed to step away from some of those church commitments, the couple found they had plenty of time to connect with each other. They became more like best friends, spending most of their free time together. Ultimately, they found a few ministries they were both passionate about, and they were able to strengthen their marriage by spending that time together while participating in the church life they loved so much.

What you believe is possible for your marriage will determine how you behave and the results you get. If your marriage is struggling, it can become good. If it's good, it can become great. If it's great, it can become exceptional. However, all of this is only possible when you believe you can make it happen and you take action to prove that belief to be true.

Take on these beliefs to develop a winning mindset for your marriage:

- I can master the art of love.
- I choose open communication with my lifemate.
- I'm committed to growing and changing for the better.
- I'm becoming selfless in my marriage.
- We overcome challenges together.
- I repel all threats to our marriage.
- I always choose forgiveness.
- I value true intimacy in my marriage.
- My lifemate is my best friend.
- I'm proud to share our marriage success with other couples.

4. Be a person of integrity.

There's no better example of learning the importance of integrity in marriage than my (Michael's) own story. When Myra and I married, I was still immature. I was a young man, but I hadn't yet put away my boyish ways. The bottom line: I was selfish. I was irresponsible and unwilling to be accountable for my behavior. I put our marriage at risk, and if I hadn't changed, I could have lost everything.

Initially, I changed my behavior because I was afraid of losing my wife. Over time, my motivation changed from one of fear to a sincere desire to make my wife happy. It became a part of my nature to be accountable to her and to go out of my way to make her feel secure. It's in my DNA now. I instinctively try to make her laugh twenty times a day to make up for those times when I made her cry. I live with integrity so I can bury all that hurt and pain with new memories, lots of laughter, and playtime when I can get it.

Don't blame external factors, including other people, for your choices and actions. Don't depend on anyone else to make it possible for you to have the kind of marriage you dream of having. Instead, develop and exercise self-control and commit to doing what you say you're going to do. Take control of the fate of your marriage.

Follow these steps to be a person of integrity in your marriage.

- Assume responsibility for your own actions.
- Honestly address your personal and relationship vulnerabilities.
- Identify three things to do each day that will make you a better lifemate.
- Get clear about your priorities and eliminate time parasites.
- Remember that just because you can, doesn't mean you should.
- Make technology work for you.
- Focus on the most important things.
- Make the most of your time.

- Focus on improving your gifts.
- Do what feels right, not just what feels good.

5. Prepare to love and be loved.

Earlier, we shared the story of Shonda (the thawed Ice Queen) and Isaiah. The pain of past hurts kept Shonda from opening up to her husband. The trauma affected the way she saw herself, the way she interacted with the world, and even the way she looked. When we started working with Isaiah and Shonda, she was stiff, tense, and rigid. There was a wall between them, but Isaiah loved his wife and they were both willing to work on the marriage.

Shonda had to give up the pains of the past in order to open up to her husband and stop making him pay the price for what she'd gone through before he entered her life. No one could reverse or undo what she'd experienced in previous relationships, but she had to find a way to break those chains. Shonda was willing to do the work, and as she released the past, the wall came down. Where there had been dark clouds, there were smiles, laughter, and joy. As Shonda experienced a revival, so did her marriage.

Don't drag old baggage into your marriage. Don't make your lifemate pay the price for the pain someone else caused you. Instead, take the time to assess what went wrong in your previous relationships, what role you played, and how you want to do things differently this time around. If you're struggling to let go of the ghost of past relationships, seek counseling to deal with any lingering hurt from adultery, abuse, or failed romance. Free yourself to love again by letting go of the past.

If marriage is supposed to be about love, as most of us believe, and Jesus was the perfect embodiment of love, then Jesus just might be the special ingredient all marriages need in order to succeed. John 13:34 teaches us that Jesus asks us to love one another as He has loved us. This love is exemplified in the fruit of the Spirit: love, joy, peace, patience, kindness, goodness, faithfulness, gentleness, and self-control (Galatians 5:22-23). If we truly love Jesus, we should follow His example and allow these gifts to manifest themselves in our lives. You probably know the song "They'll Know We Are Christians By Our Love." Christian marriages should be living testimonies of the power and love of Jesus Christ. (Regardless of the faith you practice, living up to God's love in your marriage is the goal.) That's a pretty high standard to meet, but the reward for completing the journey makes it worthwhile.

As your LifeM8Z mentors, we invite you to consider re-dedicating yourselves to Christ by reaffirming your commitment to love your spouse more intimately and more intensely, as God loves you. We challenge you to make a renewed commitment to release the awesome potential of the seeds of love that God has sown into the heart of your marriage. Sow the seeds of encouragement, trust, forgiveness, edification, fidelity, and love. God will bless you immensely, and the light of your love will radiate more brilliantly for all to see.

6. Set boundaries, prune past relationships, and survive deployment.

Patricia married Marlon after he'd already joined the military, and she thought she knew what to expect—until they faced his first deployment. Then, Patricia realized she'd totally underestimated how difficult that separation would be. Marlon was in a remote location, where he couldn't always make their scheduled calls, and the silence caused Patricia's imagination to run wild. She knew her husband lived and worked alongside women who had deployed with him, and the thought made her uncomfortable. She loved and trusted Marlon but worried about him spending so much time with female co-workers. When she expressed her concern, Marlon felt like it was impossible to prove he was faithful to her.

We encouraged Marlon and Patricia to work together to set boundaries and to define their rules of engagement. That included doing whatever was possible to treat their calls as sacred while Marlon was deployed. Marlon had to demonstrate that he understood how important that time to connect was to their marriage. He had to allow his wife to dote on him and express her concern while he was away. At the same time, Patricia stopped obsessing over her doubts about her husband's fidelity. By making those changes, they each made deployment easier for the other to manage.

The reality of military life is that there will be times when you and your lifemate are physically separated from one another. However, even when there are thousands of miles between the two of you, distance doesn't have to cause an undue strain on your relationship. Your marriage can continue to thrive and grow stronger even when video chat is your main form of communication. In order for that to happen, you have to be proactive and prepare for it in advance.

It's imperative that you set clear boundaries so the only friendships in your life are with people who support you in your marriage. Sever ties or minimize communication with romantic partners from your past and anyone who could pose a threat to your marriage because of their belief system or their feelings for you or your lifemate. Set yourselves up for success well before you face deployment and work together to make sure the deployment goes smoothly and your reunion is an amazing celebration.

7. Accept the LifeM8Z challenge.

While each of these couples focused on different areas of struggle in their marriage, they all embraced the seven skills we share here. The ways they applied them were unique to their situation, but these skills set them all up for success. These couples have become living examples of the hard work and the heart work of marriage.

The first six skills we've shared with you only work if you put them into practice. This final skill, taking on our two-step challenge, will make it easier for you to regularly practice all of the others. The first step in the LifeM8Z challenge is for you and your lifemate to check in with each other regularly. Once a week, sit down for a hand-in-hand, eye-to-eye, knee-to-knee conversation. Take this moment to reconnect. Ask each other simple questions like:

- How are you doing this week?
- What has really surprised you this week?
- What pleased you?
- Have I done anything to annoy you?
- What have I done that pleased you?
- How's your love tank? Is it filled?
- What three specific things can I do to move your love tank closer to full?

Neither of you can expect the other to read your mind. Instead, regularly ask and answer these types of questions to make it easier to meet each other's needs.

The second step of the challenge is to take time each week to pray the prayer we shared earlier in this book, ask these questions, and seek God's guidance.

- *What do I need to do* to become a better man or woman?
- *What do I need to do* to become a better husband or wife, a better Christian (or Muslim, Jew, or Buddhist, etc.), and a better friend and partner to my lifemate?

- *What do I need to change* to become a better husband or wife, a better Christian (or Muslim, Jew, or Buddhist, etc.), and a better friend and partner to my lifemate?

- *What do I need to sacrifice or give up* to become a better husband or wife, a better Christian (or Muslim, Jew, or Buddhist, etc.), and a better friend and partner to my lifemate?

- *What commitments do I need to make or rededicate myself to* in order to become a better husband or wife, a better Christian (or Muslim, Jew, or Buddhist, etc.), and a better friend and partner to my lifemate?

In our work, we see many struggling marriages, but we also see rock-solid marriages that don't rise to the level of lifemates. They're doing all the "right" things—running the household, raising the kids, excelling in their careers—but they're missing the fruit of the Spirit. They're missing the joy and passion of being best friends and playmates. When you take the LifeM8Z challenge, you commit to continuously improving the depth and quality of your relationship while intentionally and persistently striving to discover higher and higher levels of love. You commit to love and passion and hard work. You commit to successfully completing the mission of marriage.

Many military couples suffer in silent pain, despair, and desperation as they watch the marriage they thought would be happily ever after wither and die. So often, they can't figure out where the relationship got off track or what they can do to fix it. If you are an Airman, Soldier, Sailor, or Marine, or a military family member and you find yourself struggling, we strongly encourage you to seek professional help from the military resources available to you. You may find guidance from a more experienced couple in your unit, the chaplain, family services, or Military OneSource. The key is to seek help.

Thank you for making time to read *Fighting for Your Military Marriage*. We've shared with you the foundation of what binds us together as LifeM8Z and the tools we use to coach and mentor couples on their way to a better marriage. If you're willing to do the work, this book will equip you with the necessary skills to make your marriage a phenomenal success. Please pay it forward by presenting a copy to another couple who you believe will benefit from it.

Now that you've reached the end of this book, we hope you will commit to a lifelong campaign to fortify your marriage. We encourage you to keep in touch with us via our website (LifeM8Z.com) and our Facebook page (facebook.com/lifem8z/).

To contact us to conduct a retreat, workshop, or speaking engagement, email us at LifeM8Z@LifeM8Z.com.

We look forward to meeting you at one of our in-person or online workshops.

About the Authors

Michael and Myra Holmes are certified professional life coaches, certified specialists in marriage enrichment, and certified prepare/enrich facilitators. Married for nearly forty years, they are the CEOs of LifeM8Z. Their mission is to guide couples in removing barriers to intimacy, commitment, passion, and love by using their tailor-made process designed to help military couples achieve successful marriages.

Michael and Myra's articles, blogs, videos, and speaking events have transformed thousands of couples. Together they serve on the board of directors of Better Marriages, are co-marriage ministry leaders at Sixth Mount Zion Baptist Temple, and volunteer with multiple organizations nationwide.

Michael earned a bachelor's in psychology at North Carolina Central University, a master's in human resource management/development at Chapman College, and served 27-years in the U.S. Air Force, retiring in the rank of Colonel.

Myra served as a dedicated military spouse and enjoys traveling, crocheting, and sewing.

Michael and Myra reside in Yorktown, Virginia, and have three wonderful daughters.

To learn more, visit www.LifeM8Z.com

CREATING DISTINCTIVE BOOKS
WITH INTENTIONAL RESULTS

We're a collaborative group of creative masterminds
with a mission to produce high-quality books to position
you for monumental success in the marketplace.

Our professional team of writers, editors, designers,
and marketing strategists work closely together to ensure
that every detail of your book is a clear representation
of the message in your writing.

Want to know more?
Write to us at info@publishyourgift.com
or call (888) 949-6228

Discover great books, exclusive offers, and more at
www.PublishYourGift.com

Connect with us on social media

@publishyourgift